The Statistical Pioneers

The Statistical Pioneers

by

James W. Tankard, Jr.

Schenkman Publishing Company Inc.
Cambridge, Massachusetts

Copyright © 1984

Schenkman Publishing Company, Inc.
190 Concord Ave.
Cambridge, Massachusetts 02138

Library of Congress Cataloging in Publication Data

Tankard, James W.
  The statistical pioneers

    Bibliography: p. 141
    1. Mathematical statistics—History. 2. Mathematicians—
    Biography. 3. Statisticians—Biography.
I. Title.
QA276.15.T36   519.5′092′2 B   81-8769
ISBN 0-87073-408-3   AACR2
ISBN 0-87073-409-1 (pbk.)

Printed in the United States of America.

To Lanie

Statisticians are still regarded as living in a world of their own and possessing very few human attributes.

Maurice Kendall
"Statisticians – Production and Consumption"

... it will never suffice to state a man's discovery; one must explain how and why he made it, and why it was he who made it, what idiosyncrasies guided or handicapped him, and so forth.

George Sarton
The Study of the History of Science

The man creates the mathematical theorem, but the events of a man's life create the man, and the three are indissoluble.

Florence N. David
Games, Gods and Gambling

Contents

Preface

This book is intended to be a supplementary textbook in statistics classes presently being taught in many fields. Its purpose is to place the major ideas of statistics in their historical setting and tell the stories of the men who developed them.

Statistics is often taught with little reference to the men who developed the basic ideas of the field. Frequently the correlation coefficient is discussed without reference to Sir Francis Galton, the chi-square test without mention of Karl Pearson, the *t*-test without a discussion of William Sealy Gosset, and analysis of variance without consideration of Sir Ronald Fisher. Even statistics textbooks typically neglect these thinkers who did so much to establish a discipline.

The Statistical Pioneers was written to show that the major ideas in statistics were developed by human beings, and to bring out their human qualities. The book should also serve the purpose of making the statistical tests themselves easier to understand by describing the practical problems they were invented to solve. Finally, the book attempts to show something of the origin of statistical ideas by locating them in the social and cultural context from which they arose.

There have been previous attempts to write the history of statistics, but they are now mostly out of date. These include: Todhunter's *A History of the Mathematical Theory of Probability from the Time of Pascal to that of LaPlace* (1865), Meitzen's *History, Theory, and Technique of Statistics* (1891), Koren's *The History of Statistics, Their Development and Progress in Many Countries: In Memoirs to Commemorate the Seventy-Fifth Anniversary of the American Statistical Association* (1918), Walker's *Studies in the*

History of Statistical Method (1929), and Westergaard's *Contributions to the History of Statistics* (1932).

Sir Maurice Kendall, a statistician and historian of statistics himself, said recently, "It seems to me that the true history of statistics has not yet been written" (1976, p. 53).

Many people apparently find statistics a cold and lifeless field, and would agree with poet W. H. Auden, who wrote, "Thou shalt not sit with statisticians nor commit a social science" (1966, p. 225). There was nothing cold and lifeless about the people who made the great discoveries in statistics, however. This book is dedicated to bringing out their struggles, their senses of humor, their strong interpersonal relationships (both positive and negative), and their passion for their work.

The following persons provided valuable assistance in the completion of this book: Ms. Anne Weakliam of the Head Brewer's Department, Arthur Guinness Son & Co. (Dublin), Ltd., who gave the author a tour of the Guinness Museum; Mrs. Eithne Mooney, Technical Information Officer, Arthur Guinness Son & Co. (Dublin), Ltd., who answered questions about Gosset and provided a copy of *Letters from W. S. Gosset to R.A. Fisher 1915-1936*; A.C. Pattison, Visits Organizer, Rothamsted Experimental Station (Harpenden, Hertfordshire, England), who arranged a tour of the Broadbalk field and a visit in the Statistics Department; and Professor Egon S. Pearson of University College London, who answered two letters asking questions about his father and other statisticians.

Introduction

The dominant research paradigm in the social sciences is the use of statistical analysis to study human beings and their society. Basically, this paradigm involves gathering quantitative data and applying a statistical test that allows the researcher to draw conclusions. The approach is widely used in research in the fields of psychology, sociology, education, political science, and communication, and has recently had an impact on traditionally non-quantitative fields such as history.

The beginnings of this paradigm can be traced back to the Belgian statistician and astronomer Adolphe Quetelet, who discovered a surprising numerical regularity in the rates at which crimes were committed, and to the English anthropologist Francis Galton, who was trying to find a mathematical expression for the laws of heredity. The paradigm was fully developed by Galton and three other English researchers – Karl Pearson, a mathematician and scientist who continued Galton's work on heredity; William Sealy Gosset (also known as "Student"), an industrial researcher who faced the problems of analyzing brewery data; and Ronald Fisher, a mathematician enlisted to analyze the data at an agricultural experiment station.

The four most widely used statistical tests within this paradigm are the *correlation coefficient*, the *t-test*, the *chi-square test*, and *analysis of variance* (see Table A). These four tests were developed primarily by four men – Galton, Pearson, Gosset, and Fisher – but it was not strictly a case of each man inventing one test. The more characteristic pattern was that one thinker initiated an idea and others added to it later.

For instance, Galton first thought of the correlation coefficient,

1

but Pearson and some of his colleagues later perfected it. Galton himself occasionally drew upon the talents of better mathematicians than himself. The chi-square test was originated by Pearson, but the degrees of freedom concept was added later by Fisher. The t-test, which did not originally have that name, was invented by Gosset around the time that he studied with Pearson, and it was later refined by Fisher. Analysis of variance was invented by Fisher, but Gosset was very close to discovering the technique and the two were corresponding frequently at the time.

There is no evidence that Galton ever met Gosset or Fisher, but there was extensive personal contact between the other pairs — Galton and Pearson, Pearson and Gosset, Pearson and Fisher, and Gosset and Fisher. Some of these relationships were quite close and pleasant, while others were less than amiable. Pearson was a great admirer of Galton, and for twenty years spent much of his spare time writing his four-volume biography. Gosset spent a year studying with Pearson, and referred to him affectionately as "the old man" even when they were disagreeing. Fisher published some of his first statistical writings in *Biometrika*, the journal Pearson edited, but the two men would later have their differences. Gosset and Fisher were close friends, exchanging a lengthy correspondence and visiting one another even though they lived in different countries.

Jacob Bronowski once wrote that statisticians are "difficult and intemperate men" (1956, p. 75). The description is certainly true of Pearson and Fisher, who fell into numerous arguments, both with other statisticians and with each other. The description does not fit Galton and Gosset, however, who were both modest and good-humored men.

To a large extent, these four men invented *statistical method* as it has come to be practiced. The value of statistical method is that it gives us a logical basis for drawing valid conclusions about a wide range of phenomena from a limited number of observations. That is why it has become the dominant paradigm in the social sciences, as well as an important technique in other fields, such as medical research. For example, statistical method has allowed us to evaluate the effectiveness of the Salk polio vaccine by studying a sample of children (Meier, 1972); determine the effectiveness of a negative income tax by studying a limited number of families (U.S. Department of Health, Education, and Welfare, 1973); and estimate the national unemployment rate on the basis of a sample (Taeuber, 1972). These tasks involve the ancient problem of *induction* — reasoning from the particular to the general — and statistics gives us a basis for doing that.

Fisher himself thought that statistics was ushering in a major new stage of thinking. He commented that geometry had led to humanity's first "great stage of intellectual liberation" by discovering the principles of *deduction*, and that *biometry* — the pursuit of biological knowledge by quantitative methods, but essentially a synonym for statistics — was leading to the second great stage by discovering the principles of *induction* (Fisher, 1948, p. 262).

At least three of the four statistical innovators – Galton, Pearson, and Fisher – appear to have been child prodigies whose precocity has been memorialized in many stories and anecdotes. All four men have also been categorized as geniuses.[1]

Despite these accolades, these four statisticians have not always been given great recognition for the ideas that they developed. Statistics textbooks almost invariably devote at least a chapter each to the correlation coefficient, the *t*-test, the chi-square test, and analysis of variance, but they often say little about the people who have created these tests. A random analysis of the indexes of selected statistics textbooks fully supports this conclusion (see Table B).[2]

Of course, these four men did not work in a vacuum, cut off from other influences. Their work built on still more fundamental ideas, including particularly the *binomial distribution*, the *normal curve*, and the *central limit theorem*. These ideas were shaped and influenced by some of the great mathematicians and scientists of earlier times, including Isaac Newton, Edmund Halley, Blaise Pascal, Pierre de Fermat, Abraham De Moivre, Pierre-Simon Laplace, Karl F. Gauss, and Adolphe Quetelet. The four statisticians were also stimulated by their contemporaries, including the biologist Walter Frank Raphael Weldon, the economist and statistician Francis Ysidro Edgeworth, and the statistician George Udny Yule, who was a student of Pearson's. In fact, the list of persons who have made important contributions to the development of statistical thinking is a fairly long one (see Table C).

The four major statisticians were also operating in a certain environment that had a great influence on their thoughts. They grew up in the country that had produced in 1660 the Royal Society of

London, with its tradition of valuing scientific thinking and the people who contributed to it. The journals and meetings of the Royal Society and other British scientific organizations made it easy for intellectuals, including the early statistical researchers, to exchange ideas. The excellent university training in the sciences available at Oxford and Cambridge was also certainly a factor. Cambridge was one of the leading world centers for mathematics training in the late nineteenth century, and Galton, Pearson, and Fisher were all products of that training.

After the Industrial Revolution, many companies were beginning to hire university scientists to help improve their products. This movement led to Gosset and Fisher's being employed by a brewery and an agricultural research station, which had begun in connection with a fertilizer production enterprise. Finally, many powerful, revolutionary ideas were beginning to circulate at this time and affected the statisticians. Darwin's theory of evolution, articulated in his *Origin of Species* in 1859, and Karl Marx's controversial doctrines in particular influenced these men.

Out of these influences came a period of intensive research activity that roughly began with Galton's discussion of the first regression line in 1877 and approximately ended with Fisher's 1923 paper presenting the first analysis of variance table. In this fifty-year period, these four men had discovered the methods that have become the standard research approach in the social sciences and in much of medicine and agriculture.

Table 1 A
Frequency of Use of Various Statistical Tests
In Journals in Psychology and Communication*

	Psychology Journals (1972)	Communication Journals (1970-1975)
	%	%
Analysis of variance	71	28
Correlation	25	33
Chi-square	15	25
t-test	12	21
Nonparametric tests	12	3
Factor analysis	4	10

Sources: Edgington (1974), *American Psychologist* 29:25; Lee and Olkes (1976), *Journalism Educator* 31, no. 3:55.

*Percentages are of those articles in the journals that used statistics. Percentages do not total to 100% because an article could use more than one statistical test.

Table 1 B
Number of Citations to Statisticians in Index
For some Widely Used Statistics Books

	Francis Galton	Karl Pearson	"Student" (W. S. Gosset)	Ronald Fisher
Guilford (1936)	15	20	0	13
McNemar (1949)	0	4	1	7
Moroney (1951)	0	0	0	0
Walker & Lev (1953)	0	6	2	16
Ostle (1954)	0	3	0	3
Mills (1955)	1	12	5	20
Snedecor (1956)	5	7	5	34
Dixon and Massey (1957)	0	0	0	0
Senders (1958)	1	1	1	2
Freund (1960)	0	2	1	0
Mack	0	0	1	0
McNemar (1962)	0	5	1	5
Hays (1963)	1	7	1	5
Yamane (1964)	0	0	0	4
Bliss (1967)	0	2	2	29
Williams (1968)	0	1	0	0
Hammond et al. (1970)	6	2	2	7
Guilford & Fruchter (1973)	2	2	1	6
Spence et al. (1976)	0	0	0	0
Wright (1976)	0	2	1	1
Wonnacott & Wonnacott (1977)	0	0	1	1
Kimble (1978)	0	0	0	0
Hopkins and Glass (1978)	0	3	1	1

This tabulation is based only on the indexes, which do not always cite all references to a name. For instance, Wright (1976) contains a discussion of Galton's *quincunx*, but Galton's name is not in the index.

The material between two commas was counted as one page citation, whether it was a single page number or several page numbers (104-106 or 92f).

A citation to "Student's *t* distribution" or the "Pearson product moment correlation" was counted as a citation for the individual. However, "*F* ratio" was not counted for Fisher, and "studentized range statistic" was not counted for Gosset.

Table 1 C
Contributors to the History of Statistics

Pierre de Fermat	1601-1665 French
John Graunt	1620-1674 English
Blaise Pascal	1623-1662 French
James Bernoulli	1654-1705 Swiss
Edmund Halley	1656-1742 English
Abraham De Moivre	1667-1754 French/English
John Arbuthnot	1667-1735 Scottish/English
Thomas Bayes	1702-1761 English
Thomas Simpson	1710-1761 English
Joseph-Louis Lagrange	1736-1813 Italian/French
Pierre-Simon Laplace	1749-1827 French
Adrien-Marie Legendre	1752-1833 French
Christian Kramp	1760-1826 French
Robert Adrain	1775-1843 Irish/American
Karl F. Gauss	1777-1855 German
Simeon-Denis Poisson	1781-1840 French
Friedrich Wilhelm Bessel	1784-1846 German
Johann Franz Encke	1791-1865 German
Adolphe Quetelet	1796-1874 Belgian
Augustus De Morgan	1806-1871 English
Auguste Bravais	1811-1863 French
George Boole	1815-1864 English
Issac Todhunter	1820-1884 English
Sir Francis Galton	1822-1911 English
John Venn	1834-1923 English
Francis Ysidro Edgeworth	1845-1926 English
Mansfield Merriman	1848-1925 American
Karl Pearson	1857-1936 English
Walter Frank Raphael Weldon	1860-1906 English
George Udny Yule	1871-1951 Scottish/English
William Sealy Gosset	1876-1937 English
George W. Snedecor	1881-19 American
Sir Ronald Fisher	1890-1962 English

1
The Early Statisticians

Statistics has evolved from "State Arithmetic," or the tabulation of numerical information about nations, to a rigorous process for making valid scientific inferences. Along the way, it has been influenced by areas as diverse as mortality record-keeping, gambling, theology, and astronomy.

The word *statistics* (or, more precisely, the German *statistik*) was apparently first used by Gottfried Achenwall, a German political geographer, in 1748 or 1749 (Hankins, 1908, pp. 480-481; Walker, 1929, p. 32). It was more or less a synonym for "State Arithmetic"; the description of the strengths and weaknesses of a nation state. At first, the word did not necessarily mean a *numerical* description of a state, although it later must have become obvious that this was the most useful form of description. These early meanings for the word *statistics* are reflected in the definitions of the word by Quetelet, Westergaard, and Moroney (Table 1.1). The more modern meaning of statistics is a method of drawing conclusions on the basis of observations.

The roots of the field of statistics can be traced back to a number of different areas. Walker (1929), Westergaard (1932), and Lundberg (1940) similarly describe three lines of evolution. According to Walker, statistics developed from: "the mathematical theory of probabilities; the growth of agencies for enumeration, calculation and measurement; and the rise of the modern state with its increasing needs for information concerning its own resources and those of its neighboring rivals" (Walker, 1929, p. 31).

Kendall (1968a) traces the development of statistics to ten sources:

> Probability theory originated at the gaming table; the collection of statistical facts began with state requirements of soldiers and

7

money; marine insurance began with the wrecks and piracy of the
ancient Mediterranean; modern studies of mortality have their
roots in the plague pits of the seventeenth century; the theory of errors was created in astronomy, the theory of correlation in biology,
the theory of experimental design in agriculture, the theory of time
series in economics and meteorology, the theories of component
analysis and ranking in psychology, and the theory of chi-square
methods in sociology. (p. 224)

Finally, certain areas of the field of statistics can be traced back
even further, to the days of the Old Testament. Stigler (1974) has
suggested that the design of experiments may be the oldest area in
statistics, and has found descriptions of experiments in the Book
of Daniel.

Some of the earliest applications of probability were in life insurance, theology, and gambling — areas perhaps not as discon-
nected as they might appear at first glance. In all three, probability
was used to make inferences about the unknown with some degree of certainty. Much of this early work in probability and statistics took place in England and France in the 1600s. In England,
scientists and mathematicians who were members of the young
Royal Society made important contributions. Mathematicians in
France, concerned with some practical problems of gambling,
brought about other developments.

English Work by the Royal Society

The 1600s were a time of scientific awakening. Some of the first
important scientific discoveries were being made by Kepler,
Galileo, Toricelli, Newton, Pascal, Robert Boyle, William Harvey,
Francis Bacon, and others. This growing interest in science led in
England to the development of the Royal Society, or, more accurately, the Royal Society of London for the Improvement of
Natural Knowledge. The Society evolved from a discussion club
which began meeting in 1645 and was sometimes known as "the
invisible college." In 1660, the group organized as the Royal Society, and received its charter from Charles II in 1662. The Society
agreed to meet weekly to "consult and debate concerning the
promoting of Experimental Learning" (Stimson, 1948).

In the early days, the Society was comprised of two-thirds
amateur and one-third professional scientists (Stimson, 1948).
Among the charter members were two pioneers in the history of
statistics — William Petty and John Graunt. Other members who

joined the Royal Society in its early years, including Edmund Halley, John Arbuthnot, Thomas Bayes, Abraham De Moivre, and Thomas Simpson, also made important contributions to the development of statistics.

Royal Society member John Graunt produced one of the first works of the State Arithmetic type in his *Natural and Political Observations Mentioned in a Following Index and Made Upon the Bills of Mortality*, published in 1662. Graunt noticed that the weekly "Bills of Mortality" in the city of London, which reported the number of burials and the causes of death, were reviewed week by week, but that nobody had examined them over a longer period. He compiled the causes of death for twenty years, placed the information in a table for easy comparisons, and then commented on his findings. For instance, he observed that only a few persons, or 86 out of 229,250, were murdered. He pointed out that this contrasted with figures from Paris, where "few nights escape without their *Tragedie*" (1662, p. 35).

Graunt also compiled the first table showing mortality rate according to age by using a crude type of estimation. He had some basis for believing that out of 100 births, 36 persons would die before the age of six. And he apparently assumed that only 1 out of 100 would still be alive at seventy-six years. He then "sought six mean proportional numbers between 64, the remainder, living at six years, and the one, which survives 76 . . ." (1662, p. 69). This resulted in the first mortality table (see Table 1.2), a collation that would become very useful later in insurance work and population studies.

Graunt's work seems to be one of the first efforts at what is now regarded as sociology.[1] Making quantitative comparisons of large groups of people and trying to draw conclusions are the same approaches used by later sociologists, such as Durkheim in his suicide study (1897).

Another early book of the State Arithmetic type was *Political Arithmetic*, published in 1690 by Sir William Petty, also a member of the Royal Society. Petty was in some ways a one-man forerunner of the modern Central Intelligence Agency. In his book, he attempted to make a quantitative assessment of the strengths of England and its two principal rivals, Holland and France. The book was written around 1677, but publication was withheld so that it would not offend France. The book dealt with the numbers of people, acres of land, numbers of ports, numbers of ships, and other measures of resources of the various countries. Petty concluded "that the King's subjects are not in so bad a condition as discontented men would make them" (p. 388).

Graunt's work on mortality tables inspired further research by Edmund Halley, a scientist best known for his discovery of the comet that bears his name. Not only was Halley able to show that a comet that appeared in 1682 was the same one that had appeared in 1607, 1531, 1456, 1301, 1145, and 1066, and that it had a period of about seventy-six years, but he was also largely responsible for prompting Newton to write his *Principia*, and helped finance the project. Halley's work on mortality appeared in *Philosophical Transactions*[2] in 1693. He began his article by crediting Graunt for his earlier work on the same subject. Halley based his mortality tables on records from Breslau, a city now in Poland but then part of Austria. Relying less on crude estimation, Halley used his tables of mortality to compute the odds that any person of a certain age would live to a particular age. He argued that the price of insurance should be different for a man of twenty, who has 100-to-1 odds that he will not die in a year, and a man of fifty, who has 38-to-1 odds that he will not die in a year. Halley's work had a great influence on the development of life insurance tables.

Another use to which probability was put during the Royal Society's early days was the attempt to prove the existence of God. Examples of this kind of effort are John Arbuthnot's (1710) argument on the basis of the regularity in the birth of the sexes and John Michell's (1767) argument regarding the clustering of stars.

In his paper, Arbuthnot looked at the number of males and females born in London for the period of 1629 to 1710, and noted that in every year there were more males born than females. Arbuthnot then computed the odds of this happening by chance if it were equally likely that males and females would be born. Here he was essentially applying the *binomial distribution,* or a form of a statistical test related to that distribution that would later be known as the *sign test.* The odds were the same as obtaining heads eighty-two times in a row while tossing a coin, or $\frac{1}{2}^{82}$. Arbuthnot argued that this consistently larger number of males is necessary because males must face danger to obtain food, and the fact that it happened eighty-two times in a row shows that it is the result of planning rather than chance. He concluded that such planning had to be done by God, and his article thus became an argument for the existence of God. According to one source, Arbuthnot's argument was adopted by theologians and preached widely (Hacking, 1965, p. 77).[3]

Arbuthnot's paper is the first known example of a statistical test. He rejected a statistical hypothesis after testing it with data. Daniel Bernoulli is reported to have used Arbuthnot's approach to statistical inference a few years later in testing a hypothesis about the inclination of the planetary orbits (Freudenthal, 1970).

Michell (1767) also used probability theory to prove the existence of God when he argued that the statistical odds were 500,000-to-1 against six stars appearing as close together as those in the constellation Pleiades by chance alone.[4]

As we have seen, theology was a major influence on the English mathematicians of this period (K. Pearson, 1926). De Moivre cites Arbuthnot's article in his famous "Approximation" paper as evidence of a divine creator, and attempts to refute a criticism by Nicholas Bernoulli of Arbuthnot's work. De Moivre used the lawfulness of statistical ratios to argue for the existence of "the great MAKER and GOVERNOUR of all." Ironically, Laplace would later argue from similar kinds of lawfulness that the hypothesis of God's existence was not needed.

Several other ties between theology and probability can be pointed out. Thomas Bayes, an active minister who was also a mathematician, became the author of Bayes's Theorem (1763). Isaac Newton was just as interested in religion throughout his life as he was in science (Westfall, 1980). The famous hospital reformer, Florence Nightingale, agreed with De Moivre that the stability of statistical ratios revealed the deity's moral purpose (K. Pearson, 1978, p. 281).

The probabilistic arguments for God's existence advanced by Arbuthnot and Michell were challenged by other thinkers. For example, John Venn (1988) characterized their conclusions as "speculations . . . which do not seem to keep quite within the limits of what is intelligible" (p.258).

French Work on Probability

While thinkers in England were concerned with mortality tables and proving the existence of God, some notable French scholars were solving certain intriguing gambling problems. One of these was called the *problem of points*. The attempts to solve this and some related problems led to some important developments in statistics.

The problem of points is concerned with the division of the stakes in a game of chance between two persons when the game has to be interrupted. Suppose two gamblers were playing a match that was supposed to go to the person winning seven games, and the match had to be stopped when player A had won four games and player B had won three games. How should the stakes be divided fairly to give player A exactly the right amount of credit for having won more games than B so far? (The problem takes various forms, but most are similar to this example.)

For more than a century this problem had perplexed mathematicians. A form of the problem was discussed in 1494 by Luca Pacioli, an Italian mathematician and friend of Leonardo da Vinci (Kendall, 1956).

The problem was presented by the Chevalier de Méré, a gambler, to Blaise Pascal, the French mathematician. Pascal was a child prodigy who attended weekly meetings of the adult French mathematicians while in his teens and had proved an important theorem in geometry at the age of fifteen. He began investigating the problem of points in an exchange of letters with Pierre Fermat, another French mathematician known for founding the theory of numbers and for inventing, simultaneously with Descartes, analytical geometry. Together, they not only solved the Chevalier's problem in their letters (1654), but at the same time they also founded the field of probability theory. Pascal and Fermat actually solved the problem of points by several different methods. One method was to use formulas that allow one to find the number of things, n, taken at a time, r. This is essentially what is known today as combination theory, or *combinatorics*.

Another technique they used to solve the problem of points was one involving the Arithmetic Triangle, or, as it is sometimes known, Pascal's Triangle (see Table 1.3).[5] The Arithmetic Triangle is easy to construct. The row across the top and the column down the left side are made up of "1"s and then each of the other numbers is the sum of the number above it and the number to the left of it. Sometimes Arithmetic Triangles are printed in a different position so that the long diagonal becomes a horizontal base upon which the triangle rests.

A means of using the Arithmetic Triangle to solve the problem of points has been described by Maistrov:

> First the number of points that each one of the players lacks to win is added. Next, the diagonal of the table is chosen such that the total number of terms in the diagonal is equal to the sum obtained. Then

the first player's part of the stake is equal to the sum of terms in this diagonal starting from 1, and the number of summands from the diagonal is equal to the number of points that the second player lacks to win. For the second player, his part of the stake is equal to a similar sum with the exception that the number of summands is equal here to the number of points which the first player lacks to win.

For example, if player A lacks three points to win, and player B four points, then $3 + 4 = 7$. We write down the diagonal consisting of 7 entries; these are: 1, 6, 15, 20, 6, 1. Hence the part of the stake belonging to A will be $1 + 6 + 15 + 20 = 42$, and the part of B is $1 + 6 + 15 = 22$. The stakes should thus be divided in the ratio $42/22 = 21/11$. (1974, pp. 46-47)

The Arithmetic Triangle also can be used to answer questions about the probabilities involved in flipping a coin. A typical problem is: What is the probability of getting three heads and one tail if I toss four honest coins at once? The answer can be found by looking at the numbers in the diagonal that is below the one corresponding to the number of coins being tossed. In this particular case, we would look at the fifth diagonal, which contains the numbers 1, 4, 6, 4, and 1. These numbers add up to 16, and they can be interpreted this way: 1 out of 16 times you would get all heads, 4 out of 16 times you would get three heads and one tail, 6 out of 16 times you would get two heads and two tails, 4 out of 16 times you would get one head and three tails, and 1 out of 16 times you would get all tails.

A similar method could have been used by Arbuthnot to find the probability of getting more male births than female births 82 years in a row if there was an equal chance of male or female. The problem is equivalent to finding the probability of tossing 82 coins and getting all heads. That probability could be determined from a large Arithmetic Triangle by going down to the 83rd diagonal and adding all 83 numbers. The probability would be 1 over that sum. The construction of a triangle with 82 diagonals would be laborious, however, and there are easier ways to solve Arbuthnot's problem.

Other more complicated problems of coin tossing can be solved with the triangle. Suppose we wanted to know the probability that in tossing ten coins, the outcome would be one of the following: four heads and six tails, five heads and five tails, or six heads and four tails. We could look at the eleventh diagonal in the triangle, and write down the eleven numbers found there. Beside each number we could write the coin outcome that it represents (see Table 1.4). Then we could add all the numbers in the triangle and get the total, which is 1024. We could next write down the probability of getting each outcome, which is its number in the diagonal divided by the total. Then we could simply add the three probabilities for the three coin toss outcomes that we had specified, and we have the answer: 0.65625. That number is the probability of getting four heads and six tails, five heads and five tails, or six heads and four tails when ten coins are tossed.

This knowledge could be very useful in various complex wagers. Someone might be in the position of placing a bet on whether a person throwing ten coins would get certain outcomes, and it would be useful information to know the odds of doing so.

The numbers found in a diagonal of the Arithmetic Triangle turn out to be fundamentally related to two important ideas in mathematics, the *Binomial Expansion* and the *Binomial Theorem*, and to an important idea in statistics. the Binomial Distribution.

The Binomial Expansion is the result obtained algebraically for taking a + b to any power. For example, the following is a Binomial Expansion:

$$(a + b)^1 = a + b$$
$$(a + b)^2 = a^2 + 2ab + b^2$$
$$(a + b)^3 = a^3 + 3a^2b + 3ab^2 + b^3$$
$$(a + b)^4 = a^4 + 4a^3b + 6a^2b^2 + 4ab^3 + b^4$$

It is apparent that the coefficients of the terms in each line of expansion are equivalent to the numbers on a diagonal of the Arithmetic Triangle. For instance, the coefficients in the first line of the expansion are 1 and 1, and the numbers in the second diagonal of the triangle are 1 and 1. Likewise, the coefficients in the second line of the expansion are 1, 2, and 1, and the numbers in the third diagonal of the Arithmetic Triangle are 1, 2, and 1. Since the calculation of these coefficients by algebra can be arduous, the Arithmetic Triangle can be very useful. Because of its relationship to these coefficients, the triangle is sometimes known as the "arithmetic triangle of the binomial coefficients" (David, 1962, p. 61).

These coefficients can also be determined by the Binomial Theorem. which is often easier than even the Arithmetic Triangle.[6]

A final note is in order on Pascal, who, like some of his British counterparts, combined probability and theology. Pascal underwent a second religious conversion soon after he had corresponded with Fermat. Pascal was in a coach that went out of control, and he was only saved from death when the traces broke as the horses plunged off a bridge. Pascal took this as a warning from heaven and largely abandoned his mathematical work for religious writing. Sometime later he formulated the famous "Pascal's wager." Pascal begins by stating that either God exists or he doesn't: which side shall we take? Pascal argues that the value of a game is the prize to be won times the probability of winning it. If God exists, the prize to be won is infinite. Therefore, even if the probability that God exists is low, we should still gamble on the side of believing that he exists, because the value is infinite, whereas the prize to be gained by believing he does not is only worldly pleasure and therefore finite (Ore, 1960, p. 416).

The Law of Large Numbers

Although Jacob Bernoulli did not solve the problem of approximating the Binomial Expansion for a large number of cases, he did draft a theorem that was another important step along the way. Bernoulli (also known as Jakob, James, and Jacques) descended from a Swiss family of mathematicians. Bernoulli wrote the first book devoted to probability, Ars Conjectandi, which was published posthumously in 1713. Bernoulli expanded the theory of combinations to the theory of combinations and permutations, and in fact coined the term permutations (Walker, 1929, p. 9). He included in Ars Conjectandi a different proof of the Binomial Theorem than Newton's, and some early thinking on many significance levels. He also introduced the expression "morally certain" for a case in which the probability is .99 or perhaps .999 (Walker, 1929, p. 10).

At this time scholars were beginning to see that probability could be applied to scientific observations, and that the probability that an observation is accurate might be related to the number of observations made. Bernoulli gave a formal proof of this intuitive notion as Bernoulli's Theorem[7] or, as it is sometimes called, the law of large numbers. This theorem, the culmination of twenty years of thought (Laplace, 1814), can be stated as follows: "As the number of observations increases, the relative number of successes must be within an arbitrarily small (but fixed) interval around the theoretical probability with a probability that tends to 1" (Ore, 1968, p. 66). Quetelet phrased it this way: "By multiplying sufficiently the number of trials, we may attain to a probability as near to certainty as we may desire – that the difference between the results of calculation and of experience may be contracted within as narrow limits as may be desired" (1849, pp. 35-36). Sometimes the theorem is given a different and more mathematically exact statement: the accuracy of observation increases inversely with the square root of the number of observations (Pearson, 1924a).

The law of large numbers can be seen at work in such present-day statistical efforts as public opinion sampling. A common problem in public opinion sampling is to estimate some proportion for a large population. For example, a researcher might want to know what percentage of the American people intend to vote for a particular candidate for president. With a sample size of 1,600, pollsters can be confident that ninety-five percent of the time their results are with ± 2.5 percent of the unknown true proportion. If they are willing to use a sample size of 50,000, as the census bureau does in determining the national unemployment rate, they can be sure that ninety-five percent of the time their results are within .45 percent of the unknown true percentage.

Bernoulli's Theorem stated in a rather general way that the more observations you make, the closer you can come to estimating an unknown quantity accurately. But his theorem did not let you compute the exact probability that your result would be within a certain range – something you could do for a small number of observations with the Arithmetic Triangle. Even the use of the Binomial Theorem becomes difficult. Researchers still needed a means of applying the Arithmetic Triangle to a large number of observations. One method of doing this would be to find a way of approximating the Binomial Expansion when the number of cases, trials, or elements becomes large. The solving of this problem led to one of the most important discoveries in statistics — the *normal curve.*

Table 1.1
Some Definitions of Statistics

Statistics has then for its object that of presenting a faithful representation of a state at a determined epoch. (Quetelet, 1849, p. 179)

The object of statistical science is to discover methods of condensing information concerning large groups of allied facts into brief and compendious expressions suitable for discussion. (Galton, 1883, p. 33)

Statistics may be regarded as (i) the study of *populations*, (ii) as the study of *variation*, (iii) as the study of methods of the *reduction of data*. (Fisher, 1925a, p. 1)

Etymologists may find the root of the word "statistics" in the Italian word *stato*, and a *statista* would thus be a man who had to do with the affairs of the State. "Statistics" would consequently mean a collection of facts which might be of interest to a statesman, whether they were given in the form of numerical observations or not. (Westergaard, 1932, p. 2)

A technique adapted to the objective recording of experience in large quantities and its meaningful analysis has, therefore, become increasingly imperative. Statistical methods constitute such a technique. (Lundbert, 1940, p. 110)

The recording of experience in terms of these [numerical] symbols and their scientific manipulation for given purposes constitute what is generally called statistics or statistical method. (ibid: p. 111)

Statistics is the branch of scientific method which deals with the data obtained by counting or measuring the properties of populations of natural phenomena. (Kendall, 1948, p. 2)

Statistical methods are concerned with the reducing of either large or small masses of data to a few convenient descriptive terms and with the drawing of inferences therefrom. (McNemar, 1949, p. 1)

Historically, Statistics is no more than State Arithmetic, a system of computation by which differences between individuals are eliminated by the taking of an average. (Moroney, 1951, p. 1)

. . . statistics is the name for that science and art which deals with uncertain inferences — which uses numbers to find out something about nature and experience. (Weaver, 1952, p. 60)

In their most significant aspect modern statistical techniques are procedures for the making of what Dewey has termed warranted assertions. (Mills, 1955, p.1)

Statistics no longer consists merely of the collection and presentation of data in tables and charts; it encompasses, in fact, *it constitutes the science of decision-making in the face of uncertainty.* (Freud, 1960, p. 3)

The theory and methods of collecting, tabulating, and analyzing numerical data compromise the study and application of statistics as the subject will be discussed in this book. (Yamane, 1964, p. 1)

. . . statistics, as I see it, is the study and informed application of methods for reaching conclusions about the world from fallible observations. (Kruskal, 1965, p. 417)

Statistics is concerned with the inferential process, in particular with the planning and analysis of experiments or surveys, with the nature of observational errors and sources of variability that obscure underlying patterns, and with the efficient summarizing of sets of data. (Kruskal, 1968, p. 206)

. . . statistics deals with some general methods of finding patterns that are hidden in a cloud of·irrelevancies, of natural variability, and of error-prone observations or measurements. (ibid: p. 208)

Statistics is the fascinating study of how you can describe an unknown world by opening only a few windows on it. (Wonnacott and Wonnacott, 1977, p. ix)

Table 1.2
John Graunt's Mortality Table

Vis. of 100 there dies		The Fourth	6
within the first six years	36	The next	4
The next ten years, or		The next	3
Decad	24	The next	2
The second *Decad*	15	The next	1
The third *Decad*	09		

Source: Graunt (1662), *Natural and Political Observations Mentioned in a Following Index and Made Upon the Bills of Mortality*, p. 69.

Table 1.3
The Arithmetic Triangle

1	1	1	1	1	1	1	1	1	1	1
1	2	3	4	5	6	7	8	9	10	
1	3	6	10	15	21	28	36	45		
1	4	10	20	35	56	84	120			
1	5	15	35	70	126	210				
1	6	21	56	126	252					
1	7	28	84	210						
1	8	36	120							
1	9	45								
1	10									
1										

Table 1.4
Computation from the Arithmetic Triangle of the Probability of Getting Four Heads and Six Tails, Five Heads and Five Tails, or Six Heads and Four Tails when Ten Coins are Tossed.

Numbers from 11th Diagonal	Outcome of Coin Toss	Probability of Each Outcome	Probability of Middle Three Outcomes
1	Ten Heads	1/1024 = .00098	
10	Nine Heads, One Tail	10/1024 = .00977	
45	Eight Heads, Two Tails	45/1024 = .04395	
120	Seven Heads, Three Tails	120/1024 = .11719	
210	Six Heads, Four Tails	201/1024 = .20508	
252	Five Heads, Five Tails	252/1024 = .24610	
210	Four Heads, Six Tails	210/1024 = .20508	
120	Three Heads, Seven Tails	120/1024 = .11719	
45	Two Heads, Eight Tails	45/1024 = .04395	
10	One Head, Nine Tails	10/1024 = .00977	
1	Ten Tails	1/1024 = .00098	

2
Abraham De Moivre and the Normal Curve

The normal curve, as mathematics historian Bryan Morgan has put it, "Is as characteristic of statistics as the hexagon is of organic chemistry or the parabola of ballistics" (1972, p. 168). It is fundamental to most of the modern statistical tests developed by Francis Galton, Karl Pearson, W. S. Gosset, Ronald Fisher, and others. The discovery of the normal curve can be traced primarily to one man, although a number of others helped extend it.

The normal curve is actually a number of different things. First of all, and most exactly, it is the line represented on a graph with x and y coordinates by the following mathematical equation:

$$y = \frac{1}{\sqrt{2\pi}} e^{-\frac{x^2}{2}}$$

One of the many astounding facts about this curve is that it involves two well-known constants from areas very different from statistics: π is the ratio of the circumference of a circle to its diameter, and e is a constant having to do with growth rates such as those involving bank interest. Secondly, the normal curve is a form that emerges when some very general problems regarding gambling procedures, such as coin tossing, are considered. This was the context that led to its discovery.

In addition, it is a form that often describes errors in measurement very well, a characteristic which led to its wide use in the observations of stars and planets in astronomy. Finally, it is a form that fits fairly closely to the measurements of many physical characteristics that are not errors at all, such as the heights of human beings, the widths of the foreheads of crabs, and counts of the number of veins in the leaves of trees.

De Moivre

The normal curve was discovered by Abraham De Moivre, a French Protestant who moved to England at the age of 21 to escape religious persecution. Although the Edict of Nantes in 1598 had given religious freedom to Protestants, it was revoked in 1685, and French Protestants lost all civil liberties. There in England, De Moivre[1] made friends with mathematicians such as Newton and Halley, and soon achieved a reputation of his own. He spent time at Newton's home, and his letters often mention conversations with Newton. In his later years, Newton is supposed to have some-times replied to questions by saying, "Ask Mr. De Moivre, he knows all that better than I do" (Walker, 1934, p. 322).

De Moivre was a religious man, and believed, as did Florence Nightingale, that the stability of statistical ratios evidenced the existence of a designing God. He thought Arbuthnot's paper on the stability of the ratios of the sexes was important, and defended it against a criticism by Nicholas Bernoulli (K. Pearson, 1978, pp. 161-162).

De Moivre made other contributions to mathematics besides his discovery of the normal curve, which he himself probably did not rate very highly. He was the acknowledged authority on *chance* during his day (Clarke, 1929), and he discovered an important theorem in trigonometry which still bears his name.

The story of De Moivre's death has been told in several different versions. De Moivre worked with infinite series, and one of the properties of some infinite series is that they converge to a certain limit. One version of the story says that De Moivre began sleeping fifteen more minutes each night until he reached twenty-four hours and then he died (Eves, 1953). Another variation states that toward the end of his life, De Moivre was forced to make his living by solving mathematical brainteasers in coffee houses, and in de-spair he simply went to sleep until he died (Morgan, 1972). It at least seems to be true that De Moivre was feeble toward the end of his life, and slept twenty hours a day (Walker, 1934). He died at 87½ after eight days in bed.

De Moivre's discovery of the normal curve (or more accurately, the normal law, since he did not draw a curve) is contained in his paper "A Method of approximating the Sum of the Terms of the Binomial $(a + b)^n$ expanded into a Series, from whence are deduced some practical Rules to estimate the Degree of Assent which is to be given to Experiments." The paper first appeared in Latin as a 1733 supplement to De Moivre's 1730 book *The Doctrine of Chances*. De Moivre himself supplied an English translation in the second edition of his book in 1738.[2]

By citing both Jacob Bernoulli and Arbuthnot, De Moivre clearly showed that he was building on their earlier work.

The problem that De Moivre was attempting to solve was the one of computing, or at least approximating, the terms of the binomial when the number of cases becomes very large. Suppose you wanted to know the probability that when you threw 1,000 coins, you would get a result somewhere between 450 and 550 heads? It is unlikely that anyone would care about the tossing of 1,000 coins per se, but a researcher might be interested in a problem of this type if, like Arbuthnot, he was making some observations in real life and testing them against the theoretical results one would get according to probability.

To solve this problem with an Arithmetic Triangle, you would need a triangle with a diagonal containing 1,000 numbers. The answer would be the sum of all the numbers on the diagonal corresponding to the outcomes in question (between 450 and 550 heads) divided by the sum of all the numbers on the diagonal. This is not practical, and researchers needed a method of approximating this ratio. These numbers on the diagonal are the coefficients of the binomial expansion, as pointed out in the previous chapter. So what we need is a method of approximating the ratio of the sum of the coefficients of the middle terms of the binomial expansion to the sum of the coefficients of all the terms. This is what De Moivre sought and found – a formula that would approximate this result for any set of middle terms that one wished to examine.

De Moivre discovered this formula through the application of infinite series and calculus. The formula he obtained was essentially the equation for the normal curve given at the beginning of this chapter, although the notation was different.

Exactly how De Moivre got from the binomial expansion to the

equation for the normal curve is not very clear in De Moivre's original paper.[3] According to De Morgan, it was the fashion then "to
publish results and conceal methods" (1838, p. vii). De Moivre's
proof is not really clarified in the descriptions of his work by
Pearson (1924a) or Walker (1929). More detailed explanations of
the derivation can be found in Peters and Van Voorhis (1940,
pp. 279-285) and Burgess (1927, pp. 249-252).

One of the points that De Moivre's paper brought out was the
basic relationship between the binomial expansion and the normal curve. This relationship can be illustrated by plotting a graph
of the data from table 1.4 in the preceding chapter, which gave the
probabilities of various outcomes when ten coins are tossed. If the
numbers of tails are plotted along the horizontal axis, and the
probability of getting any number of tails is plotted along the ver-
tical axis, then the graph looks very much like a normal curve
(Fig. 2.1). As the number of coins being tossed becomes larger and
larger, the shape of the plotted points becomes more and more like
a normal curve.[4]

The credit for discovering the normal curve is often given to
Laplace or Gauss rather than De Moivre. The normal distribution
is sometimes even referred to as the *Gaussian distribution*. Because De Moivre was the first person to compute the areas under
the normal curve at 1, 2, and 3 standard deviations, however, he
appears to deserve the credit. Pearson (1924a) concurs, arguing
that De Moivre, and not Laplace or Gauss, should get credit for the
discovery. His position seems to be the prevailing one.

A number of different terms have been applied to the normal
curve throughout history. It has been called the *error curve* and
the *probability curve*. When the normal curve is applied to a set of
scores arranged in a frequency distribution, the term *normal distribution* is often used. The idea that measurements should follow
the normal curve has been referred to as the *law of error*, the *normal law of error*, the *normal law* and the *Gauss-Laplace law of
frequency of error*.

The first use of the term "normal curve" apparently is not
known. Galton may have been the first person to do so; he clearly
used it in *Natural Inheritance* (1889, pp. 54-55). Walker (1929)
says the term might go back to Quetelet, but does not cite any definite place that he used it. Seal (1967) gives Galton credit for coming up with the name "normal law," but Maistrov (1974) attributes
the same term to the French mathematician Henri Poincaré. Pear-

son wrote that "many years ago I called the Laplace-Gaussian curve the *normal* curve" (1920, p. 185), but it seems clear that he did not originate the term.

It is also difficult to identify the person who actually *drew* the first normal curve. Thomas Bayes included a figure resembling a normal curve in his classic paper introducing Bayes's Theorem in 1763, but he was dealing with a different distribution than the normal (Sheynin, 1971). Laplace describes in his *Theorié analytique des probabilités*, published in 1812, the process of drawing a curve representing the errors around a mean (Todhunter, 1865). De Morgan provided a set of instructions for drawing a normal curve and included drawings of normal curves of different shapes. He didn't call it the normal curve, however, but "the curve which exhibits the law of error" (1838, p. 133). In addition, Quetelet included in his 1849 book on probability a number of histograms which fit the shape of the normal curve.

Simpson

A researcher working in the direction of drawing the normal curve, but who did not quite succeed, was Thomas Simpson, the English mathematician. Simpson was interested in the problem of errors of observation — a very practical problem of the time being faced particularly by astronomers. When astronomical observations were repeated — the measurement of the ascension of a star, for instance — the repeated measures did not exactly agree. What was the best value to use for that measure? It seems obvious today that the best solution is to take the average or mean of the varying measures, but this apparently was not a widespread practice. A paper by Simpson argued the usefulness of taking the mean of a number of observations. He concluded his paper by saying:

> Upon the whole of which it appears, that the taking of the Mean of a number of observations, greatly diminishes the chances for all the smaller errors, and cuts off almost all possibility of any great ones; which last consideration alone, seems sufficient to recommend the use of the method, not only to astronomers, but to all others concerned in making of experiments of any kind (to which the above reasoning is equally applicable). And the more observations or experiments there are made, the less will the conclusion be liable to err, provided they admit of being repeated under the same circumstances (1755, pp. 92-93).

At this same time, there was also considerable speculation about the shape of the distribution of errors about a mean. While some people suggested that it might be a rectangle, which would mean all errors were equally likely, others recommended a circle (Walker, 1929). Simpson suggested that it might be a triangle, with the errors "respectively proportional to the terms of the series 1, 2, 3, 4, 5, 6, 5, 4, 3, 2, 1: which series seems much better adapted than if all the terms were to be equal, since it is highly reasonable to suppose, that the chances for the different errors decrease, as the errors themselves increase" (1755, p. 91).

Simpson reprinted his paper with some additions in his 1757 collection entitled *Miscellaneous Tracts on Some Curious and Very Important Subjects in Mechanics, Physical-astronomy, and Speculative Mathematics*. One of the additions was a diagram for the triangular error distribution. Simpson's triangle was certainly a better approximation to the distribution of errors than a circle or a rectangle. It was someone after Simpson — probably Laplace — who demonstrated that the normal curve provides a very good fit to the distribution of errors. Astronomers were to make great use of the normal curve in the next 150 years. A typical distribution of errors in astronomical observation, taken from publications of the Royal Society at Greenwich and reported by Quetelet (1849), is shown in Fig. 2.3.

Simpson's work introduced another new element into statistical thinking. De Moivre's efforts dealt only with the probabilities of events that either occurred or did not: either a tossed coin shows a head, or it does not; either a new birth is a male, or it is not; and so on. The word "binomial" brings out this two-valued characteristic, and events of this type are said to be described by the binomial distribution.

When we discuss errors in measurement, however, we are talking about a different kind of distribution. Many measurements can vary continuously — that is, they can take on any value of an infinite range of values. This kind of distribution is known as a *continuous distribution*, which Simpson was the first to deal with (Kendall, 1961).

It is not clear how much Simpson was influenced by De Moivre's work. Simpson's 1755 paper does not cite De Moivre. The two knew each other, however. Simpson wrote a book on annuities, a topic on which De Moivre was the acknowledged expert, which led to some criticism of Simpson's work by De Moivre

(Clark, 1929). David (1962) accuses Simpson pointblank of plagiarizing from De Moivre's *Doctrine of Chances*.

Laplace

The application of the normal curve to errors of measurement was largely the work of the great French mathematician Pierre Simon Laplace and of the esteemed German mathematician Carl Friedrich Gauss. These gentlemen did much to popularize the normal curve, although neither should get credit for its discovery.

Laplace was a mathematician, astronomer, and physicist, and a friend of Napoleon's. He is known for his work on celestial mechanics, which showed that the universe is deterministic and follows mathematical laws. He saw the potential for applying De Moivre's work to determining the error rate of various types of measurements, and began to use this approach regularly.

Laplace was apparently applying the principles of probability to the discussion of errors of observation as early as 1774 (Merriman, 1884). He used the method to deduce the shape of the earth from measurements of arcs of meridians and pendulum observations.

Laplace made several other contributions to statistics. He stated the first proof of the *Central Limit Theorem*, made some of the first attempts at representative sampling from a population, and did some of the earliest work using multiple linear regression. One writer has claimed "that Laplace was more responsible for the early development of mathematical statistics than was any other man" (Stigler, 1975, p. 503).

Most of Laplace's writings are difficult to follow. Like Ronald Fisher a hundred years later, Laplace often omitted steps in his reasoning. Fisher used the word "evidently"; Laplace frequently wrote "it is clear that . . ." in place of long and difficult calculations (Fréchet, 1968, p. 23). Laplace's full treatment of probability, *Theorié analytique des probabilités*, is known for its difficulty — De Morgan called it the "Mont Blanc of mathematical analysis" (Stigler, 1975, p. 507). A more accessible source for Laplace's statistical thinking is his *Philosophical Essay on Probabilities* (1814), an attempt at popularization in which he deliberately avoided any formulas.

In the *Essay*, Laplace discusses the need in astronomy and other sciences of going beyond Bernoulli's general statement that the greater the number of observations, the more the results approach the truth. What is needed is a means of estimating the *precision* of the obtained results, or the probability that the obtained results are within a certain range of the true value. Laplace then gives the following explanation of the formula for the precision of the results, and it seems to be essentially a statement in words of De Moivre's formula:

> When we have thus obtained the exponential which represents the law of the probability of errors, we shall have the probability that the error of the result is included within given limits by taking within the limits the integral of the product of this exponential by the differential of the error and multiplying it by the square root of the weight of the result divided by the circumference whose diameter is unity (1814, pp. 76-77).

Laplace applied his formula to a number of problems, including an attempt to estimate the population of France. He based his estimate on birth rate information gathered from thirty districts throughout France. He computed the ratio of the population to annual births in these districts, and then multiplied that figure times the number of annual births in France. This gave him an estimated population of France in 1802 of 28,352,845. Using his formula to compute a margin of error, he concluded that the odds were 300,000-to-1 that the error was as large as half a million (Laplace, 1814). Westergaard, while questioning the accuracy of this calculation, says modern representative sampling procedures "are in reality greatly indebted to Laplace" (Westergaard, 1932, p. 83). In addition, Laplace (1814) applied his formula for margin of error to Bouvard's calculation that the mass of Jupiter was equal to 1/1071 of the mass of the sun, and concluded that the chance was 1 in 1,000,000 that the result was in error as much as 1/100.

In 1810, Laplace proved the Central Limit Theorem, the idea that extends the usefulness of the normal distribution even further and gives it a central place in sampling theory and hypothesis testing. Statistician Alexander Mood has written of the Central Limit Theorem: "It is the most important theorem in statistics from both the theoretical and applied points of view. And it is one of the most remarkable theorems in the whole of mathematics" (1950, p. 136). The Central Limit Theorem can be stated as follows:

> Suppose that a multitude of equal-sized random samples are gathered from the same infinite population. The sum of each sam-

ple is computed and the sums of the different samples are put together to form a new distribution. It follows that the new distribution is normal. (An assumption is that the random samples yielding the sums are large enough.) (Weinberg and Schumaker, 1962, p. 114)

The importance of this theorem is that it explains why the normal curve is so pervasive in nature. Many kinds of measurements that we can make must be comprised of sums of various independent influences operating simultaneously.

The amount of error in an astronomical observation, for instance, must be the sum of a large number of tiny forces. Some of these would be at work in the measuring instrument. The vernier gauge attached to the telescope, and every individual part linking it to the telescope, could all contribute a small amount of error. Other tiny influences on error would come from the observer – the person's state of fatigue, the distracting thoughts of the moment, and the like. The Central Limit Theorem tells us that all these separate influences would add up in such a way that the distribution for a large number of errors would follow the normal curve.

A variation of the Central Limit Theorem is called the *Central Limit Theorem for Means*. It states:

Suppose that a multitude of equal-sized random samples are gathered from the same infinite population. The mean of each sample is computed and the means of the different samples are put together to form a new distribution. It follows that the new distribution is normal. (An assumption is that the random samples yielding the means are large enough.) (Weinberg and Schumacher, 1962, p. 117)

This variation of the theorem is important because it means that certain statistical tests will work *even if* the distribution of raw scores being dealt with is not normal. Many statistical tests are made on *means* of samples. And the Central Limit Theorem tells us that the distribution of means – upon which the statistical test is based – tends to be normal even when the distribution of underlying scores is not. This makes it possible to compute the very precise estimates of probability necessary for statistical tests.

Actually, De Moivre had anticipated the Central Limit Theorem to some extent. His proof that the binomial distribution tends toward the shape of the normal distribution as a sample grows larger was a special case of the Central Limit Theorem – that special case in which every independent influence being considered could add either a 1 or a 0.

Laplace was involved in other statistical studies. He investigated the ratio of the sexes at birth, and, like Arbuthnot, found a regular tendency in favor of boys. The ratio for France was 16 boys to 15 girls. Laplace, an atheist and a determinist, did not see this as "proof of Providence," however, but merely an indication of some regular cause at work (1814, p. 70). In addition, Laplace was one of the first researchers to use multiple linear regression, applying it to such problems as determining whether or not the moon had effects on barometric pressure readings (Stigler, 1975, p. 510).

Gauss

Carl Friedrich Gauss, one of the three or four greatest mathematicians of all time, also did much to promote the normal curve.

Gauss was a mathematical genius who, at the age of three, detected an error in his father's calculations of the wages of an employee. Gauss studied at the University of Gottingen, and later became professor of astronomy and director of its observatory. At some point in Napoleon's advances, Laplace is reported to have told him to spare Gottingen because "the foremost mathematician of his time lives there" (Dunnington, 1955, p. 251).[5]

Gauss was also active in areas besides mathematics. He and the physicist Wilhelm Weber invented an electromagnetic telegraph in 1833, some years before Morse did. They transmitted over a distance of about 8,000 feet from Gauss's observatory to Weber's laboratory.

Gauss has been given credit for discovering the normal curve by a number of writers. These include Merriman (1884), Bronowski (1973), and Stewart (1977), as well as in the article on Gauss in the *Encyclopaedia Britannica* (15th ed., *Macropaedia*, Vol. 7, p. 967). Nevertheless, his role with regard to the normal curve appears to be one of establishing and popularizing rather than discovering. He did formulate a different derivation of the normal law from De Moivre's, a variation which was used in some of the first widely used statistics texts, such as that of Merriman (1884).

The most stunning accomplishment Gauss achieved through the use of statistics was to predict the location of a missing new minor "planet" (asteroid), which he did by using the *method of least squares*. The minor planet that Gauss relocated was Ceres, the largest asteroid in the solar system and the first to be discovered. It was first spotted by Giuseppe Piazzi of the Palerno Observatory on January 1, 1801. He observed it for forty-one days, after which it disappeared from view. Only a few observations of the position of the asteroid existed, but by using the method of least squares, Gauss was able to estimate its orbit. Ceres was rediscovered during the period of November 25 to December 31, 1801, at almost exactly the place Gauss predicted. Several astronomers participated in the rediscovery, including Heinrich Wilhelm Matthaus, Wilhelm Olbers, and Franz Zach. Gauss apparently achieved an advantage over other mathematicians by having discovered the method of least squares in 1795. Although he did not publish it, because Adrien-Marie published it first in his *Nouvelles méthodes pour la détermination des orbites des comètes.* (1805), he is usually credited with the method's discovery.

Some of Gauss's friends and colleagues also made important contributions to statistics. One of his students, Johann Franz Encke, completed a work in 1832 that contains formulas for the standard error of the mean and the standard error of a standard deviation. His work is a likely prospect for the first statistics textbook (Walker, 1929).

A friend and fellow astronomer of Gauss's, Friedrich Wilhelm Bessel, introduced the term *probable error,* which Gauss quickly began to use (Walker, 1929). The probable error was a measure of precision much like the standard deviation used today. The probable error is that deviation from the mean containing between its positive and negative values one half of the observations. In other words, it is an even 50-50 bet that a randomly picked observation will fall within the distance of plus or minus the probable error from the mean. The term was used widely by later writers, including De Morgan, Quetelet, and Galton. The probable error has an exact relationship to the standard deviation as it is used today — it is 0.6745 times the standard deviation. This number appeared in many statistical formulas before 1900. Although De Moivre had used the concept of probable error in his additions in 1738 to his 1733 paper, he had not given it this name (Walker, 1929).

In 1829, one of Gauss's visitors at the observatory was Adolphe Quetelet, the Belgian astronomer (Dunnington, 1955). Quetelet was making measurements of terrestrial magnetism, and the visit stimulated Gauss to do research on magnetism. We do not know whether the two discussed statistics, but since both made important contributions to that field, it is tempting to imagine that they did.

Quetelet

Adolphe Quetelet was an astronomer who has been called the founder of sociology (Landau and Lazarsfeld, 1968) and, indeed, the founder of statistics (Sarton, 1935). In addition to popularizing statistics in Belgium and other countries, Quetelet was also one of the founders of the Royal Statistical Society of London in 1834.

Quetelet studied mathematics, received his doctorate after completing a dissertation on conic sections, and became founder and head of the Royal Observatory at Brussels. In 1823, the Belgian government sent Quetelet to Paris to study astronomy during his stay. He also spent some time working with Laplace. Greatly impressed with probability theory, he seems to have concluded that the statistical approach was the best way to study anything, including human society. In *A Treatise on Man* (1842), his major work on human society, Quetelet discussed such concepts as *disturbing forces, perturbations, centres of gravity,* and *constant causes,* ideas directly influenced by Laplace's writing on celestial mechanics.

Quetelet began collecting statistical data on society relating to many topics — births, deaths, robberies, illnesses, murders, suicides, and so forth. He was struck by "the remarkable constancy with which the same crimes appear annually in the same order" (1842, p. 6). This regularity is indicated by one of his tables in *A Treatise on Man* dealing with murders (Table 2.2).

Quetelet interpreted this regularity as evidence that there was a basic lawfulness underlying human behavior. He noted that the rates of crime are often constant in the same location year after year, but that they will differ from place to place. This observation led him to the radical conclusion that the causes of crime lie not in the individual but in society. Quetelet realized, though, that this idea raised some difficult problems about free will. He wrote, "This possibility of assigning beforehand the number of accused and condemned persons which any country will present, must give rise to serious reflections, since it concerns the fate of several thousand men, who are driven, as it were, in an irresistible manner, towards the tribunals, and the condemnations which await them" (Quetelet, 1842, p. 83).

In another table in *A Treatise on Man*, Quetelet lists the probabilities of being convicted for various types of persons (Table 2.3). This effort was conducted in 1842 and is similar to present studies of judicial bias. Quetelet's *A Treatise on Man* is full of these tables reporting sociological data. Many of them are two-way and three-way cross tabulations, a method widely used in modern sociology.

Quetelet also did pioneering work by taking the normal curve, which the Paris astronomers had applied to errors in measurement of the stars, and applying it to measurements of human beings. Much of this work is reported in his *Letters Addressed to H.R.H. the Grand Duke of Saxe Coburg and Gotha, on the Theory of Probabilities, as Applied to the Moral and Political Sciences.* In one study published in the *Edinburgh Medical Journal*, Quetelet measured the chests of 5,738 Scotch soldiers, and concluded that the measurements fit the law of probability – the normal curve – quite well (Fig. 2.4).

Quetelet thought that this distribution of the measurements of 5,738 chests shows no more variation than would 5,738 chest measurements taken on the same individual. He appears to have argued that Nature was attempting to produce an ideal type and that the variation in chest measurements represents errors by Nature. This line of thinking was probably an attempt to create a strong logical relationship between the measurement of errors in astronomy and Quetelet's new use of the normal curve. However, it seems to have placed him in the rather odd position of charging God with error.

Quetelet also originated the concept of the *average man*, or "l'homme moyen." He argued that the average man "is in a nation what the centre of gravity is in a body" (Quetelet, 1842, p. 96). The average man was the ideal in beauty and goodness, whom nature was striving to produce, but couldn't because of various interfering factors. This notion of the "average man" has a number of problems, however. A person could be average in some ways, but noticeably nonaverage in other ways (Kruskal, 1968). It is also easy to think of dimensions, such as kindness, in which the average might not be the ideal of goodness and beauty.

In another study that shows an ingenious use of the normal curve, Quetelet examined the height measurements of 100,000 conscripts for the French army, and discovered some interesting evidence of fraud. He found that, in general, if the measurements were arranged by one-inch intervals, they formed a normal curve. But there was a peculiar deviation from normality in the section of the curve containing the lower heights. A person had to be five feet two inches tall in order to serve in the French army. The theoretical prediction from the normal curve is that 26,345 men out of 100,000 should be less than five feet two inches tall. The measurements from conscripts showed 28,620 falling in this category, or 2,275 more than theory would predict. Furthermore, the next two categories of height – 61.821 to 62.884 inches and 62.884 to 63.974 inches – showed a deficiency of about 2,114 cases from the number they should have according to the normal curve. This number is very close to 2,275, the number of excessive persons found in the lowest height category. Quetelet concludes, "Is it not a fair presumption, that the 2,275 men who constitute the difference of these numbers have been fraudulently rejected?" (1849, p. 98). Apparently a number of young Frenchmen were not very patriotic when the time came for their draft physicals; they bent their knees to avoid the draft.

Quetelet's bold assertion that the measurements of heights of human beings were appropriately described by a "Law of Error" did not go unchallenged. John Venn, the English logician, wrote:

> When we perform an operation ourselves with a clear consciousness of what we are aiming at, we may quite correctly speak of every deviation from this as being an error; but when Nature presents us with a group of objects of any kind, it is using a rather bold metaphor to speak in this case also of a law of error, as if she had been aiming at something all the time, and had like the rest of us missed her mark more or less in almost every instance. (1888, p. 42)

Venn pointed out that the Law of Error was being applied by Quetelet and others to three very different observations: (1) the various combinations afforded by games of chance (and represented by the successive terms of the binomial expansion); (2) measurements of many kinds of natural objects, such as heights; and (3) errors in measurement, or in target shooting. Despite his apparent challenge, Venn goes through several lines of reasoning and seems to conclude that the same mathematical law does apply to all three. In fact, the Central Limit Theorem provides justification for this summation.

However, the question Venn raised is still a controversial one in some quarters. As recently as 1960, biologist Lancelot Hogben argued, "There is indeed no justification for the analogy between natural variation and instrumental error, unless we invoke a supernatural agency" (p. 271).

Table 2.1
De Moivre's Values and the Corrext Modern Values for the Areas under the Normal Curve at 1, 2, and 3 Standard Deviations (σ's) from the Mean

	De Moivre	true value
1 σ	.341344	.341345
2 σ's	.47714*	.47725
3 σ's	.49937	.49865

Source: Pearson (1924a), Biometrika 16:403.

*Pearson actually reports values of .95428 and .95450 for 2 standard deviations and .99874 and .99730 for 3 standard deviations, but this would include the area on both sides of the mean, whereas for 1 standard deviation he has reported the area on only one side of the mean.

Table 2.2
Rates for Murders and Types of Murders in France for Six Different Years

	1826	1827	1828	1829	1830	1831
Murders in general	241	234	227	231	205	266
Gun and pistol	56	64	60	61	57	88
Sabre, sword, stiletto, poinard, dagger, etc.	15	7	8	7	12	30
Knife	39	40	34	46	44	34
Cudgels, cane, etc.	23	28	31	24	12	21
Stones	20	20	21	21	11	9
Cutting, stabbing, and bruising instruments	35	40	42	45	46	49
Strangulations	2	5	2	2	2	4
By precipitating and drowning	6	16	6	1	4	3
Kicks and blows with the fist	28	12	21	23	17	26
Fire	—	1	—	1	—	—
Unknown	17	1	2	—	2	2

Source: Quetelet (1842), A Treatise on Man and the Development of His faculties, p. 6.

Table 2.3
Probability of Being Condemned (Convicted) in Court for Accused Persons in Various States (Conditions)

State of the Accused Person	Probability of being Condemned
Possessing a superior education	0.400
Condemned who has pleaded guilty	0.476
Accused of crime against person	0.477
Being able to read and write well	0.543
Being a female	0.576
Being more than 30 years old	0.586
Being able to read and write imperfectly	0.600
Without any designation*	0.614
Being a male	0.622
Not being able to read or write	0.627
Being under 30 years of age	0.630
Accused of crime against property	0.655
Condemned in absence, or for non-appearance	0.960

Source: Quetelet (1842), A Treatise on Man and the Development of His Faculties, p. 104.

*This category apparently presents the average probability for all types of persons.

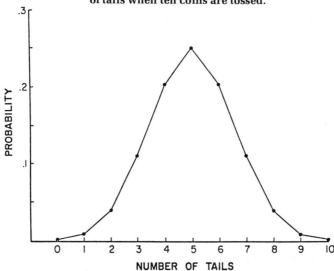

Fig. 2.1
Probabilities of getting various numbers
of tails when ten coins are tossed.

Figure 2.2
Galton's *quincunx*, a device for demonstrating the natural occurrence of
the normal curve. Also known as a "Galton board."

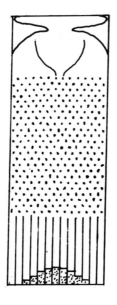

Figure 2.3
Observations of the right ascension of the Polar Star, taken from publications of the Royal Observatory of Greenwich.

Source: Quetelet (1849), *Letters . . . on the Theory of Probabilities . . .*, p. 85.

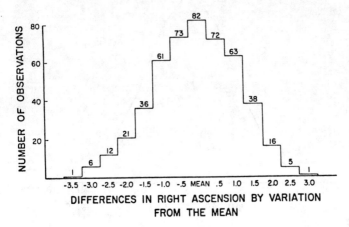

DIFFERENCES IN RIGHT ASCENSION BY VARIATION
FROM THE MEAN

Figure 2.4
Measurements (in inches) of the chests of 5,738 Scotch soldiers.

Source: Quetelet (1849), *Letters . . . on the Theory of Probabilities . . .*, p. 276.

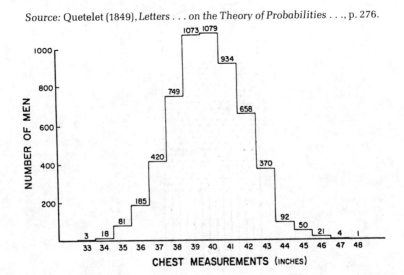

CHEST MEASUREMENTS (INCHES)

3

Sir Francis Galton and Correlation

Francis Galton was one of those Victorian Englishmen wealthy enough to be able to devote their lives to the study of science. His first cousin, Charles Darwin, who greatly influenced Galton, was another of these somewhat eccentric gentlemen scientists. Bronowski has described these men as "observers of the countryside, bird-watchers, clergymen, doctors, gentlemen of leisure in country houses" (1973, p. 291).

Galton first achieved scientific fame as an explorer of Africa in the "Dr. Livingston" mode. During his diverse career, he invented spectacles that could be used to read underwater (1865a), experimented with stereoscopic maps that would have the appearance of a three-dimensional model (1865b), and wrote a paper about receiving intelligible signals from neighboring stars (1896). Galton was something of a rarity – the dabbler in science who came up with a revolutionary discovery.

Darwin's book *Origin of Species* led Galton to study heredity in human beings, the dominant idea of his life. While trying to find a mathematical expression for the laws of heredity, Galton discovered the correlation coefficient – a technique that has since been used in thousands of studies. The origins of the still-raging nature-nurture controversy over I.Q., and indeed the concept of I.Q. itself, can be traced back to Galton's work on heredity in human beings. (Block and Dworkin, 1976).

The same trail, which began with his reading of *Origin of Species*, eventually led Galton to the controversial notion of eugenics, the attempt to improve the human race through selective breeding. Karl Pearson, a major statistician himself and Galton's principal biographer, wrote, "We can see that his researches in heredity, in anthropometry, in psychometry and statistics were not independent studies, they were all auxiliary to his main object — the improvement in the race of man" (1924b, p. 86).

Quetelet was the other major influence on Galton besides Darwin, and much of Galton's work can be seen as a direct extension of Quetelet's. Galton took the normal curve, which Quetelet had applied to physical measurements of human beings and had made slight steps toward applying to "moral" characteristics, and extended it to mental measurement. Again, this connected with his principle belief – that mental and moral characteristics in human beings are inherited.

Fisher has pointed out that "to Galton . . . variation of all kinds had an appeal, or a fascination" (1948, p. 262). For instance, throughout his life, Galton had a strong tendency to count things. Pearson (1924b) said Galton seldom went for a walk or attended a lecture without counting something. Forrest said Galton had a "counting mania" that was almost obsessional (1974, p. 183). On one occasion when he was attending a lecture, Galton began counting the number of fidgets per minute by audience members and looked for variation when they were attentive versus when they were bored. He published a paper on the result in the journal *Nature* (Galton, 1885a). Later in his life, on two different occasions when he was having his portrait painted, Galton counted the number of brush strokes per hour. He multiplied this by the number of hours he sat, and concluded that each painting took 20,000 strokes (Galton, 1905). He once conducted a "beauty" survey of the British Isles by classifying girls he passed on the streets as either "good," "medium," or "bad" by fingering a recording device in his pocket. According to him, London ranked highest for beauty and Aberdeen lowest (1908).

Given this tendency to quantify, perhaps it was only natural that when Galton began to think about the workings of heredity, he did so in a quantitative way. By doing this, be became the founder of a new field – biometrics, the study of biology by quantitative methods. Surprisingly, Galton was not very confident of his own mathematical abilities and often turned to experts for assistance.

Early Years

Galton was born near Sparkbrook, Birmingham, in 1822, as was Gregor Mendel, another student of heredity. Galton's paternal grandfather, Samuel John Galton, was a successful businessman with an interest in science and, according to Galton, "a decidedly statistical bent, loving to arrange all kinds of data in parallel lines of corresponding lengths, and frequently using colour for distinction" (1908, p. 3). His maternal grandfather, Dr. Erasmus Darwin, was grandfather to Galton by his second wife and to Charles Darwin by his first wife. Galton's father, Samuel Tertius Galton, was a banker with that same family interest in science his own father had exhibited. His house contained microscopes, telescopes, and barometers, and he frequently used a slide rule.

Galton is thought to have had one of the highest I.Q.s ever known. Terman studied documents concerning Galton's childhood and concluded that between the ages of three and eight, Galton had "an intelligence quotient not far from 200" (1917, p. 209). In comparison, the highest I.Q. Terman had found at that time in studies of thousands of children in California was 170. Terman based his conclusion on the fact that, as a child, Galton routinely accomplished feats done by the average child when they were more than twice Galton's age. For instance, he read a small book, *Cobwebs to Catch Flies*, at two-and-a-half and was able to tell time at age four in contrast to the average child who did these things at ages nine or ten. Galton's sister, Adèle, was an invalid, and she began educating him as her special project when he was still very small. She had exposed him to the *Iliad* and the *Odyssey* before his fifth year.

Since Galton's parents wanted him to become a doctor, like his grandfather Erasmus Darwin, he began the study of medicine in hospitals in Birmingham and London. In these studies, Galton set broken limbs and performed tooth extractions. The first tooth he pulled broke in half. Galton, who wrote his father about the experience, told the young boy that the tooth was a double one and that he still had to take out the other half. The youth wouldn't let him work on it, however. When Galton started tugging on another tooth, the boy "bolted straight out, cursing all the Hospital Doctors right manfully" (Pearson, 1914, p. 102).

Galton was not happy with the study of medicine. He felt that "the medical knowledge to which I had access was very lax and that its progress seemed barred" (Pearson, 1914, p. 199). Later in his life, Galton suggested a way that medical knowledge could be extended through a statistical approach, unknowingly seconding Louis's practices:

I wish that hospitals could be turned into places for experiment more than they are, in the following perfectly humane direction. Suppose two different and competing treatments of a particular malady: I have just mentioned a case in point. Let the patients suffering under it be given the option of being placed under Dr. A or Dr. B, the respective representatives of the two methods, and the results be statistically compared. A co-operation without partisanship between many large hospitals ought to speedily settle doubts that now hang unnecessarily long under dispute (1908, p. 44).

The French clinician Pierre-Charles-Alexandre Louis was already using medical experiments to show that bloodletting and blistering were ineffective as treatments (Spink, 1978, p. 13).

Cambridge

After his experience in hospitals, Galton enrolled at Trinity College, Cambridge, in 1840 to continue his education. At the time, Cambridge was one of the world's centers for advanced thinking and training in mathematics. Having shown an aptitude for math during his first year, Galton then studied with the mathematician and geologist William Hopkins. Hopkins was famous for successfully preparing students for the mathematical tripos, or exam, given every year at Cambridge. The top performers on the test every year were known as wranglers, and the best was called the first or senior wrangler. High wranglers in the Cambridge tripos often went on to distinguished careers in science or other fields. Among the high wranglers coached by Hopkins were physicist George Gabriel Stokes, physicist William Thomson (Lord Kelvin), physicist James Clerk-Maxwell, and mathematician Isaac Todhunter.[1] Sir George Biddell Airy, the Astronomer Royal of England and John Couch Adams, who, in conjunction with the Frenchman Leverrier, discovered the planet Neptune, were also high wranglers.[2]

Galton also studied with one of the great English mathematicians, Arthur Cayley, while Cayley was a student. Galton spent his second long vacation from Cambridge traveling with a group of students, and Cayley was one of two tutors who went along. He graduated from Cambridge in 1842 as senior wrangler, and was awarded the Smith's Prize in mathematics immediately afterward. After a career as a lawyer, during which he published in mathematics, Cayley returned to Cambridge as a professor. His great contributions to mathematics were inventing matrix algebra and being one of the originators of the geometry of n-dimensional space. Galton wrote of him:

> I was, in a very humble way, able to compare the work of various mathematical teachers with that of Cayley. The latter moved his symbols in battalions, along broad roads, careless of short cuts, and he managed them with the easy command of a great general (1908, p. 72).

There is some evidence that Galton might not have applied himself to his studies at Cambridge. He wrote, "E. Kay . . . , afterwards Lord Justice of Appeal, had rooms on the same staircase as myself, and we wasted a great deal of time together, both in term and in my second summer vacation" (1908, p. 69). Furthermore, Galton's health broke down. "I had been much too zealous, had worked too irregularly and in too many directions, and had done myself serious harm" (1908, p. 79). He had to stop preparing for the mathematical tripos, and ended up taking a Poll Degree, a degree without honors.

Around the time that Galton graduated from Cambridge, his father died. He thus found himself "with a sufficient fortune to make me independent of the medical profession" (1908, p. 82). He happily abandoned any intention of practicing medicine and decided to travel. His next five years have been characterized as "the fallow years" (Pearson, 1914, p. 196). Galton journeyed to Egypt and Syria, but Pearson says they were "the restless visits of the well-to-do young man, seeking travel-pleasure in the routine way, without scientific object and without archaeological or linguistic knowledge" (Pearson, 1914, p. 197).

First Scientific Successes

At this time, explorers were just beginning to map Africa, the "Dark Continent," and Galton became attracted by the adventure promised there. This time he went to the Royal Geographical Society before leaving, and found out which areas would be useful to explore. Galton departed on April 5, 1850 for a two year trip. He visited the interior of South Africa and mapped its unknown regions. His findings were summarized in *Tropical South Africa*, published in 1853. In the following year, Galton received a Gold Medal from the Geographical Society for his exploration of Africa. This recognition established him as a member of the scientific world and, along with subsequent work, led to Galton's election as a fellow of the Royal Society in 1856.

While vacationing at Dover in 1853 with his mother and sister Emma, he attended a Twelfth Night party, and met Louisa Butler, whom he married the same year. Four years later, the Galtons moved to 42 Rutland Gate, a house in London near Hyde Park where they would live for the rest of their lives. The house still exists in an area now populated by ambassadors and the wealthy, and bears a plaque pointing out that Sir Francis Galton, explorer, statistician and founder of eugenics "lived here for fifty years."

The next few years until 1865 were spent in various types of scientific dabbling, particularly in the fields of geography and meteorology. He published the *Art of Travel* in 1855 and received a note of thanks from Charles Darwin for sending him a copy. He also became acquainted in the mid 1850s with William Spottiswoode, the mathematician and geographer who later served as president of the Royal Society. Galton planned to go on a surveying trip to the Sinai peninsula with Spottiswoode, but had to withdraw because of a throat abscess. However, he did go on an expedition with George Airy, the Astronomer Royal, to see a total eclipse of the sun visible in Spain on July 18, 1860.

Galton seems to have invented the questionnaire as a research device in 1861 when he queried meteorologists throughout Europe. He was gathering weather data, in an attempt to develop better weather maps. One of his contributions to meteorology was the term *anticyclone*. Galton and Spottiswoode also helped the London Times print its first weather maps. In 1863, Galton invented some stereoscopic maps for use in geography. He commented, "Good models, and therefore stereoscopic maps made from them, give a far better idea of a mountainous country than any ordinary map can do, however cleverly it may be shaded" (1908, p. 265).

Interest in Heredity

Some time prior to 1865, Galton became interested in heredity, his life's major research topic. His cousin's book, *Origin of Species*, published in 1859, had a strong impact on him. Galton wrote Darwin that reading *Origin of Species* had "formed a real crisis in my life; your book drove away the constraint of my old superstition as if it had been a nightmare and was the first to give me freedom of thought" (Pearson, 1914: plate II). He comments in *Memories of My Life* that the views then held on heredity were vague and contradictory, with most authors agreeing that animals inherited physical and mental qualities but being unwilling to say the same about human beings. He states, "I was encouraged by the new views to pursue many inquiries which had long interested me, and which clustered round the central topics of Heredity and the possible improvement of the Human Race" (1908, p. 288).

Bronowski has called the theory of evolution by natural selection "the most important single scientific innovation in the nineteenth century" (1973, p. 308). The challenge of testing this theory became a major life's task not only for Galton, but also for Karl Pearson and the biologist Walter Frank Raphael Weldon, and led eventually to some of the most important developments of statistics.

Other elements might have contributed to Galton's late-developing interest in heredity, including the infertility of his own marriage (Forrest, 1974). Another factor might have been Galton's friendship with Herbert Spencer, a sociologist who was writing about evolution before Darwin and who had coined the phrase "survival of the fittest." Galton and Spencer went to horse races together, and Spencer helped Galton compose a questionnaire to study the influence of heredity on members of the Royal Society.

Galton's first work on heredity was a two-part article in *Macmillan's Magazine* in 1865. It reported a study of biographical dictionaries, and the results were presented in a summary percentage table. In this early paper Galton was already taking a strong stand on the role of heredity writing, "Everywhere is the enormous power of hereditary influence forced on our attention" (p. 163).

The Normal Curve

The impact of Quetelet on Galton's thinking first appears in Galton's major work dealing with heredity, his book *Hereditary Genius* (1869). Quetelet's *Letters . . . on the Theory of Probabilities* had been made available in an English translation in 1849. In *Hereditary Genius*, Galton reprinted a number of Quetelet's tables of data that fit the normal curve, and he discussed the work on 5,738 Scotch soldiers and 100,000 French conscripts. Sarton says Galton "was deeply impressed" by his reading of Quetelet (1952, p. 6), and David believed that "Galton's obsession with the normal curve . . . can only have stemmed from Quetelet" (1968, p. 49). Pearson has disputed that Quetelet greatly influenced Galton, noting that "he formed no collection of his books, and the few references to Quetelet in Galton's writings are such as might easily arise from indirect sources" (1924b, p. 12). It does not seem likely that the reprinted tables in Hereditary Genius could have come from indirect sources, however. Sarton (1952) points out that later in his life Galton himself tended to minimize Quetelet's influence on him. In his autobiography (1908), Galton said he first became interested in the "Law of Error" (normal curve) through Spottiswoode, who had used it in a geographical memoir to discuss the probability of the elevations of certain mountain chains being due to the same cause. The index to Hereditary Genius does not mention Spottiswoode, while it does cite Quetelet. Galton also pointed out in various places that the normal law had been developed by thinkers prior to Quetelet. In Hereditary Genius (1869, p. 382), he gave credit to Laplace, and in his autobiography (1908, p. 299), he gave credit to Gauss.

In Hereditary Genius Galton took the step that Quetelet had never quite taken – the application of the normal curve to mental phenomena. Galton has described in Memories of My Life the moment when it occurred to him that the normal curve could be applied to the study of heredity. This was the point at which the two great influences on his thinking – Quetelet and Darwin – came together. Galton wrote:

> As these lines are being written, the circumstances under which I first clearly grasped the important generalisation that the laws of Heredity were solely concerned with deviations expressed in statistical units, are vividly recalled to my memory. It was in the grounds of Naworth Castle, where an invitation had been given to ramble freely. A temporary shower drove me to seek refuge in a reddish recess in the rock by the side of a pathway. There the idea flashed across me, and I forgot everything for a moment in my great delight (1908, p. 300).

Pearson (1924b) has also argued that this incident referred to the discovery of correlation rather than the idea that the normal curve could be applied to matters of heredity. Cowan has disagreed, pointing out that Galton had used "statistical units" in other works to refer to statistical values in general (1972, p. 517). Hilts (1973) has also disagreed with Pearson. It appears that Cowan and Hilts are correct. On the page of Memories of My Life before the one quoted above, Galton used the same exact phrase, "deviations expressed in statistical units," but he is clearly referring to the normal curve, not correlation. He wrote, "Deviations expressed in statistical units are usually found to conform with much closeness to the results of a certain theoretical law, discovered by Gauss, the great mathematician, and properly called by his name, though more familiarly known as the Normal Law" (1908, p. 299).

In *Hereditary Genius*, Galton discusses Quetelet's ideas and then presents his results showing that measurements of chest and height fit the normal curve. He argues, "Now if this be the case with stature, then it will be true as regards every other physical feature – as circumference of head, size of brain, weight of grey matter, number of brain fibres, etc.; and thence, by a step on which no physiologist will hesitate, as regards mental capacity" (1869, pp. 31-32). Galton is basing his argument on a close correspondence between the physical and the mental. He apparently believed, for instance, that the larger the head, the more intelligent the person.

Galton tested the fit to the normal curve of a set of examination scores for admission to the Royal Military College at Sandhurst (Table 3.1) and concluded, "It will be seen that column B [theoretical scores from the normal curve] accords with column A [actual scores] quite as closely as the small number of persons examined could have led us to expect" (1869, p. 32). This is the only place in *Hereditary Genius* where Galton fits the normal curve to data from actual testing of mental ability. However, Pearson (1924b) has said that, tested by modern methods, the Sandhurst scores did not fit the normal curve very well, and that even at the time of his writing it had not been shown conclusively that intellectual ability is distributed according to the normal law.

Galton then went on in *Hereditary Genius* to develop a rather primitive type of I.Q. scale. He devised a "classification of men according to their natural gifts" that corresponded to the normal curve and had sixteen categories. These ran from "A" to "G" for persons above average, with "G" being the highest in ability, and from "a" to "g" for persons below average, with "g" being the lowest end. There are also a class of "X" for all cases above "G" and a class of "x" for all cases below "g."

Galton reflected on how the scale might apply to different races, and concluded that Negroes were two grades below whites in intellectual abilities (1869, p. 338). In this line of thinking, he anticipated psychologist Arthur Jensen (1969), the contemporary writer on race and I.Q. Jensen has even been referred to as "Galton's Ghost" (Miller and Buckhout, 1973, p. 163).

Galton next applied the normal curve in other works, including *Natural Inheritance* (1889), where he showed that eighteen sets of measurements of human beings fit the curve reasonably well. These data came from the Anthropometric Laboratory that Galton set up as part of the International Exhibition of 1884. In *Natural Inheritance*, Galton also undertook a theoretical discussion of why something like height should be distributed according to the normal curve. This discussion is where he introduced his quincunx, or, as it is sometimes known, Galton board, earlier described in Chapter 2. Galton argued that human height is not a "simple element," but is the sum of the thicknesses of more than a hundred bodily parts (pp. 83-84). He suggested that each of these parts corresponds to a pin in the quincunx, with some tending to lengthen the stature and others to shorten it. This argument is essentially a form of the Central Limit Theorem – that sums of random selections from many independent elements will be normally distributed. The quincunx is basically a physical demonstration of the Central Limit Theorem.

While he was discussing the normal curve in *Natural Inheritance*, Galton paused to criticize the term "probable error." He said the term was "quite misleading" because it does not refer to what it seems to, the most probable error, which would be zero (pp. 57-58). He suggests that the term "Probability Deviation" be substituted, opening the way for Pearson to later introduce the term *standard deviation*. This term has a meaning slightly different from but related to the meaning of the old "probable error."

The normal curve alone did not lead Galton directly to the goal he was seeking – the discovery of the laws of inheritance. But it became a basic tool of his thinking and led him to develop statistical methods of his own for measuring heredity.

Throughout his life Galton remained a true believer in the normal curve, writing in *Natural Inheritance*: "I know of scarcely anything so apt to impress the imagination as the wonderful form of cosmic order expressed by the 'Law of Frequency of Error.' The law would have been personified by the Greeks and deified, if they had known of it" (1889, p. 66).

Regression and Correlation

Galton's book *Hereditary Genius* argued – as the title indicates – that intelligence is inherited. The evidence for this had primarily come from counting the relatives of eminent people who were also eminent. Galton needed to find a better method of showing a definite link between high or low " ability" in one generation and high or low ability in the next. Trying to find a means of showing this link led Galton to the invention of *correlation*.

Galton wanted to study the workings of heredity in human beings, but it was difficult to get careful data concerning successive generations of people. Darwin and Sir Joseph Hooker suggested to Galton that he study sweet peas, and Galton's first paper dealing with regression (which layed the groundwork for correlation) reported data from sweet peas. These results were described in an unpublished lecture entitled "Typical Laws of Heredity in Man" given to the Royal Institution on February 9, 1877. Galton investigated the relationship between diameter of parent seed and diameter of offspring seed in a sample of sweet peas. His attempt to find a measure of this relationship produced what we would today call the *regression slope* (Pearson, 1930a). He introduced the symbol r, which stood for *reversion*, and which was later used as the symbol for the correlation coefficient. Galton apparently drew the first regression line to represent this relationship in a personal notebook now in the Galton Archive (Cowan, 1972), although he did not include it in his lecture. Pearson has taken the sweet pea data and replotted the regression line (Fig. 3.1).

Galton thought he had found in the sweet pea experiments an explanation of why populations stay the same overall for generation after generation. He had been bothered by the idea that children's heights vary slightly from the heights of their parents, which implies that among the children of a gigantic couple, there should be some children even more gigantic (1908, p. 300). If this were so, how could the distribution of height for the population remain stable for generation after generation? Galton suggested that the answer was *reversion*, or the tendency of children of extremely tall (or extremely short) parents to revert back to the mean for the population.

Working with sweet peas gave some promising results, but what Galton really needed to test further his notions of heredity was data from human beings. One method he used to acquire this information was to offer prizes for family records (Pearson, 1920). Realizing that statistical records of fundamental characteristics such as height and weight did not exist for the British people, he also proposed to construct an Anthropometric Laboratory as part of the 1884 International Exhibition. This project was completed, and thousands of people had measurements taken of their keenness of sight, hearing, color sense, judgment of the eye regarding the length and perpendicularity of lines, breathing power, reaction time, strength of pull and squeeze, force of blow, span of arms, height standing and sitting, and weight. Galton said his measuring equipment had to be sturdy and easy to understand; "the stupidity and wrongheadedness of many men and women being so great as to be scarcely credible" (1908, p. 246). He reports that the device for measuring strength of blow was broken several times, and some people sprained their wrists.

Galton himself spent some time working in the Anthropometric Laboratory, and the story is told of the famous British statesman W. E. Gladstone's visit. Galton, who had a rather large head, was apparently measuring Gladstone's when this exchange took place: "'Have you ever seen as large a head as mine?' Gladstone said to Galton, on which the latter observed: 'Mr. Gladstone, you are very unobservant!'" (Pearson, 1924b, p. 379). Galton himself similarly recounts the tale in *Memories of My Life*:

> Mr. Gladstone was amusingly insistent about the size of his head, saying that hatters often told him that he had an Aberdeenshire head – "a fact which you may be sure I do not forget to tell my Scotch constituents." It was a beautifully shaped head, though low, but after all it was not so very large in circumference. Of those persons whom I have mentioned in the foregoing chapters, the heads of William Spottiswoode and Mr. Gassiott were larger round; Professor Sharpey's was the largest of all (pp. 249-250).

The Anthropometric Laboratory gave Galton vast quantities of measurement data, much of it from parents and their children. This material was very useful for continuing his investigations of regression and correlation, and Pearson has said this data led directly to the discovery of correlation (Pearson, 1924b).

After the sweet pea lecture of 1877, Galton spoke on regression again in 1885 (Galton, 1886a). The new data came from measurements of stature from human parents and offspring. Galton had drawn a table with heights of parents (averaged for the two, and called "mid-parents") on one axis and heights of offspring on the other (Fig. 3.2) in order to express the relationship between their heights. Galton writes of a moment of insight similar to the time he realized that statistics could be applied to heredity:

But I could not see my way to express the results of the complete table in a single formula. At length, one morning, while waiting at a roadside station near Ramsgate for a train, and poring over the diagram in my notebook, it struck me that the lines of equal frequency ran in concentric ellipses (1908, p. 302).

What Galton had seen is what we term the *normal correlation surface*. This is a three-dimensional figure that, if sliced vertically, produces cross sections that look like normal curves. Galton might have been aided in seeing the three-dimensional correlation surface in a two-dimensional diagram by his earlier work on stereoscopic maps. It is also possible that Galton was inspired to think of a three-dimensional correlation surface from his familiarity with Vauthier's contour map of Paris and Lalanne's three-dimensional contour form for expressing temperature data (Beniger and Robyn, 1978).

Galton did not feel that he had the mathematical training to write the formula for the surface he had found, although he knew the formula existed. He presented the problem in an abstract form to J. D. Hamilton Dickson, a mathematician at Cambridge. Galton realized that the problem was a general one and that it "might be expressed in a form that had no reference to heredity" (Galton, 1886a, p. 57). Without much difficulty, Dickson was able to provide the solution that Galton had predicted which showed that the relationship between two variables could be expressed mathematically. This proof became the basis of the correlation coefficient.

A few years later, in 1888, Galton published "Co-relations and Their Measurement, Chiefly from Anthropometric Data." This was the first place Galton used the word *correlation*, although the term had been used before by biologists in a different sense. This paper suggests that r be used henceforth as a measure of "the closeness of co-relation" (p. 145) and reports the first correlations ever determined. Pearson commented, "Galton's very modest paper of ten pages from which a revolution in our scientific ideas has sprung is in its permanent influence, perhaps, the most important of his writings" (1930a, p. 56).

Galton had been troubled by another problem with the regression approach that developed from his sweet pea research; in relating two different variables, such as height and weight, the slope of the regression line is partly a function of the units that are chosen. In a sense, this made any regression coefficient somewhat arbitrary, and not a very good measure of the relationship. But by the time of his 1888 paper, Galton had solved that problem also. His solution was to measure each variable in units of its own variability (such as the standard deviation, although Galton used the quartile). If this is done, the slope of the regression line becomes the correlation coefficient (Pearson, 1930a).

Galton's technique for determining the first correlations was to plot on a graph a number of points measured in quartile units for the two variables, draw a line that fit them best, and then find the slope of the line. He did not have a computational formula worked out; this Karl Pearson did later.

Galton presented more correlations and discussed both correlation and regression in the book *Natural Inheritance* (1889). Here Galton gives two possible explanations for the occurrence of regression. The first "is connected with our notions of stability of type, and of which no more need now be said" (p. 104). He is apparently referring to Quetelet's belief that Nature attempts to preserve the "type," or the average. Galton's second explanation is that regression results because the child inherits partly from parents and partly from ancestors, and ancestors, if traced back far enough, will have the same distribution of heights as the general population.

It is not clear whether Galton ever understood that regression was to some degree a statistical artifact rather than a demonstration of heredity at work.[3] Yet there are two reasons for thinking that Galton might have understood this. First, Dickson's calculations had shown that regression was purely mathematical, and would occur with any kind of variables when there was a less than perfect correlation. Secondly, in his paper "Regression towards Mediocrity in Hereditary Stature" (1885b), Galton presents not only the coefficient of regression for predicting height deviation of offspring from height deviation of parents (which is about two-thirds), but also the coefficient of regression for predicting height deviation of parents from height deviation of offspring (about one-third). The first coefficient indicates that tall parents are likely to have children that are not quite as tall as they are. But the second coefficient indicates that tall children are likely to have parents that are not quite as tall as they are. It is difficult to determine whether Galton fully understood these implications. Cowan (1972) argues that Galton did understand that the coefficient was the product not of heredity but of his own statistical manipulations, and that this is why he changed the name from the first term he used, *reversion*, to the second term he used, *regression*. Cowan argues that *reversion* implies heredity while *regression* does not, but the dictionary offers biological definitions for the two terms that are very much alike.

There is at least one indication that Galton did not fully understand the nature of regression.[4] The 1885 "Mediocrity" paper also contains a regression chart with the following labels: "When Mid-Parents are taller than mediocrity, their Children tend to be shorter than they" and "When Mid-Parents are shorter than mediocrity, their Children tend to be taller than they." A fuller report might have brought out the following statements, which are equally true: "When Children are taller than mediocrity, their Mid-Parents tend to be shorter than they" and "When Children are shorter than mediocrity, their Mid-Parents tend to be taller than they."

This two-way nature of regression – that it applies not only in predicting from parents to children but also in predicting from children to parents – is one of the hardest aspects to grasp, but it is also one of the strongest indications that regression is a statistical fact rather than a hereditary one. A concise discussion of this two-way nature of regression can be found in Campbell and Stanley (1966, pp. 10-12).

There has been some controversy over whether others had discovered correlation before Galton. Walker (1929) says five people – Laplace, Gauss, G.A.A. Plana, Rober Adrain, and Auguste Bravais – studied the normal correlation surface prior to Galton. But she points out that they were approaching it from a different direction; they were interested in the probability of the simultaneous occurrence of two errors, which is expressed by the same mathematical surface. Pearson (1896) initially gave credit to Bravais for discovering correlation, but later changed his mind, stating that "Bravais has no claim, whatever, to supplant Francis Galton as the discoverer of the correlational calculus" (Pearson 1920, p. 188). Apparently his reasoning is the same as that given above – that Bravais was not interested in the relationship between two variables but in the distribution of errors influenced by two independent sources.

Other Interests

Galton made other contributions, some important and some

merely interesting, in his long and varied career. He was apparently the first person who studied twins to measure the separate effects of heredity and environment (1875). These twin studies led him to conclude that nature was stonger than nurture. Today twin research is still important in studies of intelligence and of the causes of diseases. For instance, they have been used recently in research on the effects of smoking (Reid, 1972).

Galton also did some interesting research using composite photographs to try to identify certain types of persons (1883). Galton thought of the idea after he was asked by a prison official to see if certain features in photographs of criminals were associated with certain types of crime (Galton, 1908). Galton might have been influenced by Quetelet in this research, since the composite photographs seem to be a good technique for finding the "mean" or "type" for a group of persons. The technique involved photographing a series of portraits one at a time on the same photographic plate after superimposing them exactly. Although the method did not succeed in identifying a criminal type, it did result in some striking composite photographs, particularly when applied to members of the same family.[5]

Galton also attempted a statistical study of the effectiveness of prayer which was published in a popular magazine in 1872 and generated much controversy. Although he argued that the clergy were a more "prayerful class" than lawyers or doctors, and therefore should live longer, the mean ages at death for the three professions were 66.42 for clergy, 66.51 for lawyers, and 67.04 for doctors. Hence he concluded that the prayers of the clergy "appear to be futile in result" (1872, p. 129).

In other varied achievements, Galton authored a book on fingerprinting (1892), developed the technique later known as the word association test (1883), and came close to discovering multiple regression while trying to relate wind velocity, dampness, and temperature to barometric pressure (1870).

Galton assisted in the founding of the prestigious British scientific journal *Nature*. Previously, he had been a coeditor along with Herbert Spencer and astronomer Joseph Norman Lockyer (the person who named "helium") of a weekly scientific journal called *The Reader*. After it failed, Lockyer became sole editor of *Nature*, to which Galton was a frequent contributor. Galton also helped to establish *Biometrika*, the journal which Karl Pearson edited for many years and which was to publish a number of important articles in statistics. In addition, Galton once helped Charles Darwin with one of his books, *The Effects of Cross and Self fertilisation in the Vegetable Kingdom* (1876). He contributed all of the statistical analysis, which Ronald Fisher later used as one of his examples in *The Design of Experiments* (1935a).

Galton's ideas were brought to America by James McKeen Cattell, an associate who had helped him set up the Anthropometric Laboratory at South Kensington (Walker, 1929). Cattell began to teach statistical psychology at the University of Pennsylvania in 1887, and later at Columbia University (David, 1968). Cattell is considered to be "the father of mentality testing in America" (Terman, 1976).

In recognition of his many achievements. Galton was knighted in 1909. Telling Pearson the news, he wrote, "A precious bad *knight* I should make now, with all my infirmities. Even seven years ago it required some engineering to get me on the back of an Egyptian *donkey!* and I have worsened steadily since" (Pearson, 1930a, p. 386).

Throughout his life, Galton remained an ardent supporter of statistics. He once wrote:

> Some people hate the very name statistics, but I find them full of beauty and interest. Whenever they are not brutalized, but delicately handled by the higher methods, and are warily interpreted, their power of dealing with complicated phenomena is extraordinary. They are the only tools by which an opening can be cut through the formidable thicket of difficulties that bars the path of those who pursue the Science of man (1889, pp. 62-63).

The Cause of Eugenics

Galton was the founder of *eugenics*, or the improvement of the human race through encouraging reproduction of the most capable and discouraging reproduction of the least capable. He coined the term in 1883 in *Inquiries into Human Faculty*. Although the cause of eugenics lay behind Galton's interest in heredity, and thus led indirectly to his statistical discoveries, it is in many ways his least attractive and least realistic idea.

Galton was a benevolent individual, but some of his remarks on eugenics sound like beliefs the Nazis would have preached. For example, he wrote, "A democracy cannot endure unless it be composed of able citizens; therefore, it must in self-defense withstand the free introduction of degenerate stock" (1908, p. 311). Before the time of Hitler, this kind of argument must have had some appeal; both Karl Pearson and Ronald Fisher became strong advocates of eugenics. Later, when Nazi propagandists began declaring similar pronouncements, the cause became tarnished.

The future of eugenics does not look too promising. Biologists Peter and Jean Medawar concluded recently that a program of positive eugenics "is neither genetically nor politically feasible" (1977, p. 47).[6]

Galton's Utopian ideal of a society built on eugenics may have been doomed to failure, but the techniques he invented for investigating the factual basis of that cause have led to a revolution in the fields of psychology, education, and medicine.

Table 3.1
Theoretical Scores from the Normal Curve and Actual Scores For 73 Candidates Taking the Admission Examination for the Royal Military College at Sandhurst

Number of Marks Obtained By the Candidates	Number of Candidates Who Obtained those Marks	
	According To Fact	According To Theory
6,500 and above	0	0
5,800 to 6,500	1	1
5,100 to 5,800	3	5
4,400 to 5,100	6	8
3,700 to 4,400	11 73	13 72
3,000 to 3,700	22	16
2,300 to 3,000	22	16
1,600 to 2,300	8	13
1,100 to 1,600	Either did	8
400 to 1,100	not venture	5
below 400	to compete, or were plucked.	1

Source: Galton (1896), *Hereditary Genius*, p. 33.

Figure 3.1
Karl Pearson's drawing of the first "regression line."

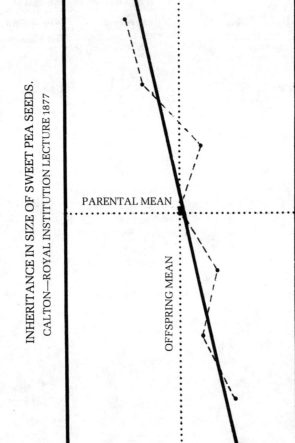

INHERITANCE IN SIZE OF SWEET PEA SEEDS.
GALTON—ROYAL INSTITUTION LECTURE 1877

Source: Karl Pearson (1930a), *Life, Letters and Labours of Francis Galton,* Vol. 3a, p. 4.
Reprinted by permission of Cambridge University Press.

Figure 3.2

Galton's table of heights of mid-parents and adult children, showing one of the concentric ellipses that led him to discover the normal correlation surface.

Source: Karl Pearson (1930a), *Life, Letters and Labours of Francis Galton*, Vol. 3a, p. 14. Reprinted by permission of Cambridge University Press.

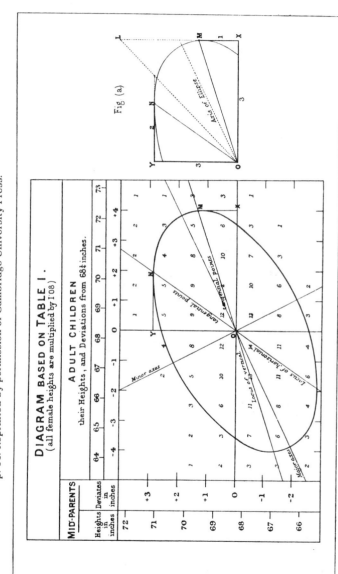

Galton's Elliptic Contour drawn from his observations.

4
Karl Pearson and the Chi-Square Test

Francis Galton can be called a Victorian scientist, but his disciple Karl Pearson was a much more complicated person and is thus more difficult to characterize. Not only did he study mathematics, but he also practiced law for a time. He made impassioned speeches on controversial subjects of the day, but then worked as a completely objective scientist. Although he was born in England, he fell in love with Germany and spoke of it as the "country of ideas" (Norton, 1978, p. 22), and later wrote to Ernst Mach that he had "for years felt himself rather German than English in both thought and expression" (Thiele 1969, p. 539). Before turning to science he wrote books on history and religion. Acclaimed as the founder of the field of statistics, he never joined the Royal Statistical Society.

Unlike Galton, an essentially benevolent man who was involved in few, if any, disputes with others, Pearson evoked either devoted friendship or extreme dislike. Among his disciples were the biologist Walter Frank Raphael Weldon, the statisticians George Udny Yule and Jerzy Neyman, the brewery researcher William Sealy Gosset (who became known as "Student"), and his son Egon Sharpe Pearson. These disciples diffused and perpetuated Pearson's ideas and made him, more than Galton, the father of statistics. Pearson's enemies included the biologists William Bateson and Lancelot Hogben, w¹ ¬ supported Mendel's views on heredity as opposed to Galton's, ι ¬ Ronald Fisher, who disagreed with Pearson over some details of the chi-square and other matters. Something of Pearson's argumentative spirit can be seen in the title of a series of pamphlets published by his laboratory – *Questions of the Day and of the Fray*. Even Pearson's closest followers, Gosset and Yule, argued with him. Yet despite their differences in style and temperment, Gosset never gave up his affection for Pearson, however, referring to him even after their disputes as "K. P." or "the old man." Pearson returned his affection, and became Galton's principal biographer.

His spirited personality is also evidenced in his beliefs in eugenics. Pearson learned of eugenics from Galton, but his views on racial improvement became much more controversial than Galton's. For example Pearson wrote many papers speaking harshly of Jewish emigrants to Britain. The American eugenicist Frederick Henry Osborn has stated that "Pearson shares the blame . . . for making possible the dreadful misuse of the word eugenics in Hitler's propaganda" (Osborn, 1978, p. 1023).

In one respect, however, the two men were quite similar. For both Galton and Pearson, the main purpose of developing statistics was to find methods of testing the theory of evolution. Pearson was able to extend statistics further because he had the high-powered mathematical ability that Galton did not. As third wrangler in the mathematics tripos at Cambridge, and a competitor in the tough Smith's Prize exam, Pearson had no need to go to other mathematicians for help. Pearson's early work dealt with the normal curve and correlation, two concepts of central interest to Galton. Pearson finished the work Galton began on correlation by developing the product moment correlation coefficient, as well as several special types of correlation coefficients. While trying to check the fit of observed data to the normal curve and other theoretical curves he invented the *chi-square test*. Pearson also gave statistics a refinement that Galton was not able to by compiling some of the first statistical tables and clarifying some of the terminology, introducing such terms as *standard deviation*, *histogram*, and *mode*.

Early Years

Karl Pearson was born in London in 1857, nine years after the London publication of the *Communist Manifesto* and two years before the publication of *Origin of Species*. These two great classics of human thought deeply affected Pearson.

Pearson's earliest memory, according to his colleague Julia Bell, was of sitting in his high chair, sucking his thumb, and having someone tell him to stop or his thumb would wither away. Pearson put his two thumbs together and looked at them. He thought to himself, "I can't see that the thumb I suck is any smaller than the other. I wonder if she could be lying to me" (Walker, 1968, p. 497). Walker says this reveals many of Pearson's later traits: rejection of authority, appeal to empirical evidence, faith in his own interpretation of data, and questioning of the morality of people whose judgments differ from his own.

Pearson's father, William Pearson, was a successful lawyer who was also interested in history, and left unpublished notes on such topics as the history of Yorkshire (E. Pearson, 1938).[1]

Cambridge

Pearson attended King's College, Cambridge, from 1875 to 1879, and studied mathematics.[2] Soon after his arrival there, Pearson asked to be excused from compulsory divinity lectures and compulsory chapel, and after receiving his father's permission, he was excused — a request which eventually led to their abolishment. The Sunday after his request was granted, Pearson surprised everyone by appearing at chapel. He was summoned to the office of a dean, who said, "You demanded to be released from attendance at chapel, and you were there yesterday!"

"No, Sir," replied Pearson, "I asked to be released from *compulsory* attendance at chapel, and I hope to be there when the spirit moves me" (K. Pearson, 1936a, p. 36).

Pearson once attended some lectures on Dante with John Couch Adams, the co-discoverer of Neptune. A few years later, Pearson was vacationing at a hotel at St. Ives, Cornwall, when "an old fashioned pair" appeared accompanied by a porter with a large skin-covered trunk on his back. Pearson recognized the couple as Adams and his wife. Witnessing the couple being turned away when he knew the hotel had rooms, he rushed up to the manageress and cried, "What have you done! You have turned away the discoverer of Neptune." "Neptune or no," the woman replied, "I am not going to have dowdies like those in this hotel!" (K. Pearson, 1936a, i. 31).

In his last year at Cambridge, Pearson took the famous Smith's Prize Examination, a tough competition in mathematics. As part of the competition, he and several other students had to appear for a day at the home of each of the four examiners, the physicist James Clerk-Maxwell and three mathematicians — Arthur Cayley, Isaac Todhunger, and George G. Stokes. Cayley had been a tutor during one of Galton's summer reading trips. Todhunter wrote a famous history of probability and was doing work on the theories of elasticity.

At Clerk-Maxwell's, the lunch conversation turned to Darwinian evolution, and Pearson spoke disrespectfully of the story of Noah's flood. "Clerk-Maxwell was instantly aroused to the highest pitch of anger, reproving me for want of faith in the Bible!" Pearson wrote. "I had no idea at the time that he had retained the rigid faith of his childhood, and was, if possible, a firmer believer than Gladstone in the accuracy of Genesis" (K. Pearson, 1936a, p. 32).

At Cayley's, the examinees were served a luncheon of sandwiches, biscuits, and a decanter of port wine. Pearson drank the port and tried to persuade the others to try some, but they barely did. A few days later, Pearson heard from a friend of Cayley's that Cayley had said only one man had appeared to enjoy his examination paper, and that was the same one who had enjoyed the port! (K. Pearson, 1936a).

When Pearson took Todhunter's exam on elasticity, there was a question on either the torsion or flexure of prisms. Pearson answered it, using what he thought was De St. Venant's proof. A few years later, in 1884, Pearson was asked by the Syndics of Cambridge University Press to finish Todhunter's book, *The History of the Theory of Elasticity*. Pearson's exam proof had been original, and Todhunter had thought it was better than De St. Venant's. He had incorporated Pearson's answer into the manuscript of his book, with a penciled notation complimenting Pearson. Referees reading the manuscript had seen the note and apparently recommended that Pearson be invited to finish the volume (ibid).[3]

As a result Pearson graduated in 1879 with Mathematical Honors. He had been third wrangler in the tripos.

Years of Searching

Pearson left Cambridge in 1879 and went to Germany to study, spending time at the Universities of Heidelberg and Berlin. The original purpose for his going is not clear; perhaps he wanted to return to the country he had visited earlier with his parents (E. Pearson, 1938, p. 5). At this time, he changed his name from Carl to Karl, either in tribute to Karl Marx or out of his general love for German ways. Pearson also became a socialist during his time at Heidelberg (Norton, 1978, p. 23).

In 1880, Pearson returned to London and began to study law. His first article, *The New Werther* was an attack on Christianity, which he published under the pseudonym Loki (E. Pearson, 1938, p. 8). In 1881, he taught mathematics at King's College London for the first two terms and began a three-year law practice. At this same time, he also engaged in literary duels with Matthew Arnold and the librarians of the British Museum (Walker, 1968) and lectured on Marx to small audiences in London (Haldane, 1957).

In 1884, Sir Alexander Kennedy, an engineering professor at University College London who knew of Pearson's work at Cambridge, persuaded him to give up law and return to mathematics, so Pearson accepted a position as a professor of applied mathematics and mechanics at University College London. This appointment gave Pearson the base of operations for his programs of research and training in statistics for the rest of his life. People coming from all over the world to study statistics with Pearson included the American educational psychologist Helen Walker and the American sociologist Samuel Stouffer. Major Greenwood, a former student, said of his teaching, "Pearson was among the most influential university teachers of his time; he took great pains to be intelligible and could hold a large audience either of students or of merely casual hearers who were without special interest in his topics" (1949, p. 683).

Despite a heavy commitment to teaching, Pearson continued to be a productive writer, producing at least 500 works over his lifetime. Stouffer once asked Pearson how he had time to write so much. "You Americans would not understand," Pearson said. "But I never answer a telephone or attend a committee meeting" (Stouffer, 1958, p. 25).

In 1885, Pearson joined with a few other progressive thinkers to form the Men and Women's Club, a group devoted to discussing the relations between the sexes. One of the women in the group was Maria Sharpe, who was later to become Pearson's wife. This club died out through lack of interest in 1889, but not before Pearson had reported on a new book he had read, Francis Galton's *Natural Inheritance*.

Pearson's original reaction to the book was negative. Later in his life, he looked back at his original copy of *Natural Inheritance* and found it marked with marginal notes expressing anger at Galton's analogies in Chapter 3 (which discusses blends of hansom cabs and four-wheelers). "But these notes were written before I had read and grasped the value of much of the later work in the book" (K. Pearson, 1930, p. 61).

Pearson apparently revised his thinking about the book rather quickly, because by March 11, 1889, he was lecturing on Galton's theory (K. Pearson, 1906). Pearson's later comments expressed nothing but praise for the book. Pearson has said he "felt like a buccaneer of Drake's days" (E. Pearson, 1938, p. 19) when he first read it; that he was "immensely excited" (K. Pearson, 1920, p. 189) by it, and that it brought "the dawn of a new day" (K. Pearson, 1924b, p. 358).

In a letter to Mach, Pearson explains that he wanted to make the biological sciences as mathematical as the science of physics, which he had also studied at Cambridge (Thiele, 1969, p. 540). While attempting to complete Todhunter's huge work on elasticity, he was also groping with problems of philosophy of science which would later find expression in *The Grammar of Science*. Quite possibly he was familiar with Lord Kelvin's dictum: "When you cannot express it in numbers, your knowledge is of a meager and unsatisfactory kind" (Kuhn, 1977, p. 178). Apparently Pearson saw Galton's concept of correlation as the key to mathematicizing the biological and social sciences. He knew that the concept of causality was too rigid for the biological sciences – that what was needed was a concept of "semi-determinism" (Norton, 1978, p. 15). What Pearson was realizing as he read Galton's *Natural Inheritance* was that correlation was just such a concept. He understood more clearly than Galton that correlation had the potential of introducing a major paradigm shift and revolutionizing the biological and social sciences.

Pearson apparently made his first personal contact with Galton through Walter F. R. Weldon, a biologist who came to work at University College.[4] Pearson was never a student of Galton's in a formal sense, he was a disciple, friend, and defender of unmatched devotion. Galton's *Natural Inheritance* had a major influence on these two young scholars – Pearson and Weldon – and within two years both of them, with Galton's help, would found the biometric movement at University College.

Influence of Weldon

It was actually Weldon who was responsible for the first paper in biometry, or the quantitative study of biology. Weldon, while working as a biologist at Cambridge, was already thinking to some extent of a statistical approach to biology before he had read Galton's book (K. Pearson, 1906). Like many biologists of the time, he was drawn to Darwin's theory of evolution and tried to think of ways to test it. Concluding that the traditional approaches of biological study would not be fruitful, he then attempted to develop a "numerical measure of species" (ibid., p. 283).

Weldon's first biometric paper (1890) extended Galton's work by applying the normal curve to measurements of 1,000 shrimp from three widely separated places: 400 from Plymouth Sound, 300 from Southport, and 300 from Sheerness. The paper was sent by the journal to Galton as a referee, who suggested some improvements in the statistics. This association marked the beginning of their relationship.

The paper tested Galton's prediction in *Natural Inheritance* that measurements of animals would fit the normal curve even when the animals were under the influence of natural selection. Galton had tested the curve mainly on measurements of human beings and certain plants, neither of which involved natural selection. Weldon's results showed a median carapace (upper shell) length for Plymouth shrimp of 250.05 thousandths of the body length, with a probable error of 4.53. The figures for Southport were 248.50 and 3.17, and the figures for Sheerness were 247.51 and 3.05. This led Weldon to conclude that "not only does the average size of the carapace differ in different local varieties, but the range of deviation from that average differs also" (p. 451). Weldon concluded his paper by stating: "It seems, therefore, that Mr. Galton's prediction is fully justified; and that (1) the variations in size of the organs measured occur with the frequency indicated by the law of error; and (2) the 'probable error' of the same organ is different in different races of the same species" (p. 453).

In his second biometric paper (1892) Weldon again dealt with measurements from shrimp, but this time the statistical technique was correlation. He used a formula for correlation that was apparently based on J. D. Hamilton Dickson's appendix to Galton's paper on the inheritance of height (Galton 1886a). Weldon also introduced in this paper the notion of *negative correlation coefficients*. Weldon found that correlations between the lengths of various organs, such as total carapace length and postspinous length, were remarkably similar for shrimp from widely different areas (Table 4.1).

Grammar of Science

At about the same time he met Weldon, Pearson was working on his philosophy of science book, The Grammar of Science (1892). This volume was based on a series of lectures Pearson was giving at Gresham College, and it attacked some concepts in physics that Pearson thought were empty, such as force, matter, ether, and the atom. One of the reasons that Galton's Natural Inheritance may have been welcome reading was that it gave Pearson a basis to attack another of these concepts – causality. He wrote later, "It was Galton who first freed me from the prejudice that sound mathematics could only be applied to natural phenomena under the category of causation" (E. Pearson, 1938, p. 19).

In The Grammar of Science, Pearson presented the idea that concepts such as atoms and ether were not realities of experience, but constructs of the physicist's imagination, and although they were useful if they helped describe his experience, they were almost certain to be replaced by better concepts as the researcher's insight expanded. In the preface to the third edition, Pearson reported that the concepts of force and matter had been discarded since his first edition, but there was "still another fetish amidst the inscrutable arena of even modern science, namely, the category of cause and effect" (1892; 1911, p. vi). Pearson stated this argument as follows:

> No phenomena are causal; all phenomena are contingent, and the problem before us is to measure the degree of contingency, which we have seen lies between the zero of independence and the unity of causation. That is briefly the wider outlook we must now take of the universe as we experience it. (1892, p. 174)

In the Grammar, Pearson offers views that are similar to those of the Austrian physicist Ernst Mach and the American physicist-turned-lawyer John B. Stallo. The following description of Mach's ideas will illustrate the similarity:

> By analyzing the origin of certain scientific ideas, he was able to show how scientists had been led to form explanations which transcended the limits of the observable; the presence of metaphysical elements in mechanics, such as the notion of "force," is thus accounted for by pointing out that mechanics came of age during a period when men were immersed in theological problems. (Janik and Toulmin, 1973, p. 137)

Pearson had read Mach's *Science of Mechanics* in 1883, the year it was published, as he acknowledged in a letter to Mach in 1897 (Thiele, 1969, p. 538). A dissertation by C. Riddle argues that the *Grammar* is "largely an attempt to impress the ideas of Mach upon the English speaking world" (Norton, 1978, p. 14). Mach apparently did not feel that Pearson was merely restating his ideas, however. He wrote in the preface to the third edition of his *Science of Mechanics*:

> In Prof. Karl Pearson (*Grammar of Science*, London, 1892), I have become acquainted with an inquirer with whose epistemological views I am in accord at nearly all essential points, and who has always taken a frank and courageous stand against all pseudo-scientific tendencies in science. (1942, p. xviii)

As a further tribute, in 1900 Mach dedicated his *Die analyse der Empfindungen und das Verhaltniss des Physischen zum Psychischen* (*The Analysis of Sensations and the Relation of the Physical to the Psychical*) to Pearson.

Pearson apparently did not know of Stallo's work when he was writing the first edition of the *Grammar*. Mach mentioned Stallo's *Concepts of Modern Physics* in his first letter to Pearson, and Pearson wrote back that he had not heard of Stallo but would look him up (Thiele, 1969, p. 537).

Pearson's volume became a classic in philosophy of science. Albert Einstein once recommended to a young scholar who came to him for tutoring in physics that he begin with Karl Pearson's *The Grammar of Science* (Clark, 1971).

Statistical Papers

Once the *Grammar* was finished, Pearson began devoting more of his time to the statistical problems Weldon was raising. Pearson's contributions to mathematical statistics came in a series of papers he began publishing in 1893. These appeared in several different journals, but most of them were numbered in a continuous series with the title "Contributions to the Mathematical Theory of Evolution" (or sometimes "Mathematical Contributions to the Theory of Evolution").

Pearson's son, Egon Sharpe Pearson, has commented on these papers:

> The main purpose of all this work was the development and application of statistical methods for the study of problems of heredity

and evolution; it would certainly be wrong to think of the Pearson of this period as concerned with the development of statistical theory for its own sake. (1938, p. 26).

For the modern reader, Pearson's early papers are lengthy and difficult. Haldane says this is because "Pearson reached his conclusions by algebraical and arithmetical methods which are now seen to be needlessly laborious" (1957, p. 432). Kendall postulates that the problem with Pearson's writing was his desire to leave nothing unsaid. He reports that Major Greenwood once said to Udny Yule (about Pearson): "He reminds me of a small boy who insists on showing you the *whole* of his stamp collection" (Kendall, 1976, p. 50). These early papers were apparently written without much knowledge of Gauss and the other Continental writers on probability (E. Pearson, 1967).

The initial paper — Pearson's very first statistical paper — gave a more advanced mathematical treatment to Weldon's Naples crab data. This paper appeared in an abstract from (1893) and then was published in its entirety in *Philosophical Transactions* (1894). One of its contributions was to introduce the term *standard deviation*. Pearson wrote, "I have always found it more convenient to work with the standard-deviation than with the probable error or the modulus, in terms of which the error-function is usually tabulated" (1894, p. 88). The *probable error,* a concept which was widely used by Quetelet, Galton, and Merriman, was found by the formula

$$\text{p.e.} = .6745 \sqrt{\frac{v^2}{n-1}}$$

in which v was a score expressed as a deviation from the mean. Pearson decided that multiplying by .6745 was an unnecessary step and didn't add any new information. He therefore introduced the new concept of standard deviation, which was given by the old formula except that .6745 was no longer included. The advantage of the probable error was that you knew exactly half the observations were within one probable error either side of the mean. Pearson apparently was willing to sacrifice that for simpler computation, since if you are primarily interested in a measure of variation, the two will work equally well. He introduced the symbol σ to stand for the standard deviation.

Weldon apparently thought that correlations this similar were an indication that the species was remaining essentially the same in the five locations, while correlations that were different in some locations might have indicated that evolutionary change was taking place. He wrote:

> A large series of such specific constants would give an altogether new kind of knowledge of the physiological connexion between the various organs of animals; while a study of those relations which remain constant through large groups of species would give an idea, attainable at present in no other way, of the functional correlations between various organs which have led to the establishment of the great sub-divisions of the animal kingdom. (1892, p. 11).

Weldon's third biometric paper (1893) extended the normal curve and correlation approach to the study of crabs. In this paper, he suggested that the measure of correlation (r) be known as "Galton's function," a name which never caught on. The paper also exposed one striking exception to the general pattern that biological measurements fit the normal curve. The exception was the distribution of the measurements of the relative breadth (forehead width) of the Naples crab. Weldon himself had the idea that the distribution could have been the sum of two normal curves. This might happen if two different species were being measured together, for instance. Weldon went through some laborious trial and error calculations to test this notion, but did not publish these results (E. Pearson, 1965).

The 1893 paper concluded with a kind of rallying cry for the application of statistics to biology:

> It cannot be too strongly urged that the problem of animal evolution is essentially a statistical problem: that before we can properly estimate the changes at present going on in a race or species we must know accurately (a) the percentage of animals which exhibit a given amount of abnormality with regard to a particular character; (b) the degree of abnormality of other organs which accompanies a given abnormality of one; (c) the difference between the death rate per cent. in animals of different degrees of abnormality with respect to any organ; (d) the abnormality of offspring in terms of the abnormality of parents, and *vice versa*. These are all questions of arithmetic; and when we know the numerical answers to these questions for a number of species we shall know the direction and rate of change in these species at the present day – a knowledge which is the only legitimate basis for speculations as to their past history and future fate. (1893, p. 329)

Weldon knew his own mathematical abilities were limited, and when he turned to mathematicians at Cambridge for assistance, they had not been very helpful. Thus in 1891, he moved from Cambridge to University College London, and met Pearson, becoming the first of many to come to him for statistical help. He presented Pearson with the Naples crab distribution problem, and Pearson's work on it led to Pearson's first statistical paper.

Weldon later conducted additional studies with crabs aimed at demonstrating the theory of evolution. This research involved testing to see if the death rate of the crabs could be related to any measurable characteristics of the organism. That is, if two variations of an organism differed only slightly in some measurable characteristic, could it be shown that one died at a faster rate than the other? Pearson considered this to be "the best manner still of testing the truth of the Darwinian theory" (K. Pearson 1906, p. 291). Most of this work was done in connection with a committee of the Royal Society formed in 1894 "for conducting Statistical Inquiries into the Measurable Characteristics of Plants and Animals." Galton was the chairman and Weldon was the secretary of this committee. Weldon described this further work with crabs in his Presidential address to the Zoological Section of the British Association for the Advancement of Science in 1898. Weldon convincingly demonstrated that the change in the forehead width of crabs in Plymouth Sound had survival value. The crabs had to adjust to the fact that the water in the sound was becoming increasingly filled with silt. Weldon conducted an experiment in which crabs were kept in water containing fine mud in suspension, a condition approximating that in the sound. He found that the mean frontal breadth of the survivors was smaller than the mean frontal breadth of the dead. Weldon speculated that a narrow frontal breadth makes the process of filtration of water more efficient.

Pearson and Weldon, now teaching at the same university, joined forces to find mathematical ways of testing Darwin's Theory of Evolution. The two men lunched together before their one o'clock lectures and talked of probability and statistics, sometimes working out problems on the backs of menus or with bread pellets as an aid to thinking. Pearson said his own "earliest contributions to biometry were the direct results of Weldon's suggestions and would never have been carried out without his inspiration and enthusiasm" (ibid., p. 284). A letter from Weldon to Galton indicates that Weldon thought early in the relationship that Pearson's approach as too much that of the "pure mathematician," but that difficulty was apparently overcome, and the collaboration worked well. (E. Pearson, 1965, p. 337).

Pearson's 1894 paper discussed the general problem of analyzing a frequency curve to see if it could be composed of two normal curves. The frequency curve for the Naples crabs was asymmetrical and double-humped, while the normal curve should be symmetrical and should have one hump. Weldon had theorized that the Naples crab distribution could be the sum of two normal curves, and had done some trial-and-error testing that had supported the notion. Pearson now undertook a rigorous investigation of this idea.

The key to Pearson's analysis of asymmetrical frequency curves into two normal curves was his finding that "a curve which breaks up into two normal components can break up in one way, and one way only" (1894, p. 74). This made it possible to find the two component curves. Pearson showed that the measurements of the foreheads of the Naples crabs could be represented by the sum of two different normal curves. He said this could have been because two different species of crabs were being measured together, or because evolutionary change was taking place in the forehead of the crab. Analysis of a symmetrical frequency curve for a shell measurement from the same crabs did not show that it was represented by two normal curves, however. This finding cast doubt on the hypothesis that two species of crabs were being measured together. Pearson concluded that the crab sample was homogeneous and not mixed and that the asymmetry of the forehead frequency curve pointed out a real differentiation in that organ. He stated in the abstract, "The Naples crabs are breaking up into two different sized families, owing to evolution in their foreheads" (1893, p. 333). Pearson pointed out that the same method could be used to determine whether evolution was taking place in other species, noting that William Bateson has found a double-humped curve for the claspers (or pincers) of Earwigs.

These early statistical papers by Weldon and Pearson were based on calculations done by hand, and since these were often quite laborious, Weldon's wife often assisted him. In 1894, the biometry group purchased its first Brunsviga calculator. Pearson mentions in a footnote to his second paper that "we have used, with much economy of time, the 'Brunsviga' calculator" (1895, p. 351).[5]

Pearson's second major statistical paper, "Skew Variation in Homogeneous Material" (1895a), came in response to an inquiry from F. Y. Edgeworth, a mathematician and Oxford professor of economics who preceded John Maynard Keynes as the first editor of *Economic Journal*. Edgeworth had some price curves with skewness and asked Pearson for help in analyzing them (E. Pearson, 1965).[6]

The "Skew Variation" paper that Pearson wrote as a result of Edgeworth's inquiry introduced the terms *histogram* and *mode*. A footnote on *histogram* states: "Introduced by the writer in his lectures on statistics as a term for a common form of graphical representation, *i.e.*, by columns marking as areas the frequency corresponding to the range of their base" (1895a, p. 339). Another footnote states, "I have found it convenient to use the term *mode* for the abscissa corresponding to the ordinate of maximum frequency" (p. 345). The paper presented a set of standard types of frequency curves that are found in dealing with different kinds of data. By a fortuitous stroke, it would also turn out that these curves fit the sampling distributions of many of the new statistical concepts to be invented in the next twenty to thirty years.

Pearson's paper on "Regression, Heredity, and Panmixia" (1896) was his first paper dealing with correlation, and it was the one in which he discussed the now famous *Pearson product moment correlation coefficient*, the most widely used method of computing a correlation coefficient. Pearson stated, "The question now arises as to what is *practically* the best method of determining r. I do not feel satisfied that the method used by Mr. Galton and Professor Weldon will give the best results" (p. 264). On the next page, he introduces the product moment formula:

> Thus it appears that the observed result is the most probable, when r is given the value $S(xy)/(n\sigma_1\sigma_2)$. This value presents no practical difficulty in calculation, and therefore we shall adopt it. It is the value given by Bravais, but he does not show that it is the best. (p. 265).

That this formula is identical to the modern product moment formula becomes clear when it is understood that S is a sign for summation, x and y are scores expressed as deviations from the means, and σ_1 and σ_2 are the standard deviation of x and y.

Pearson concluded the paper with another statement of the need for a statistical approach to evolution:

At present, all this memoir proposes is to show that such subjects as inheritance, regression, assortative mating, and panmixia, are capable of perfectly directed quantitative treatment, and that such treatment, and not somewhat vague discussion of individual instances or of metaphysical possibilities, is what alone can settle the chief problems of evolution. What is wanted is a wide extension of the experimental and statistical work of Mr. Francis Galton and Professor Weldon. (p. 318).

Pearson also included in the 1896 paper several other formulas for computing the correlation coefficient. A number of them appeared in an article by Symonds (1926), who has listed fifty-two formulas for finding the Pearson product moment correlation coefficient. The name "coefficient of correlation," which came to replace Galton's "Index of Co-relation" and Weldon's "Galton's Function," was introduced in 1892 by Edgeworth (K. Pearson, 1920).

The product moment correlation coefficient was actually first published in a paper by G. Udny Yule, a brilliant young scholar who joined the Pearson group in 1893. Yule became Pearson's demonstrator and student. The product moment correlation coefficient first appeared in print in one of Yule's papers on pauperism (1895), where full credit for it was given to Pearson. Yule went on to make many original contributions and write one of the first widely used statistics textbooks. He was also the first to derive the *partial correlation coefficient*, which he called the "net coefficient," and which was described in his second paper on pauperism (1896).

Developing the theories of correlation still further, Pearson introduced the idea of *spurious correlation* (1897). Pearson seemed to be referring to the rather special case of correlations of indices made up of two variables when two such indices share a variable (for example, the ratios of femur length to humerus length and of tibia length to humerus length). The term has since taken on a more general meaning describing a relationship between two variables that appear to be causally linked but are not.

The Chi-Square Test

Pearson's paper introducing the famous chi-square test was published in 1900. The chi-square test has been called "one of Pearson's greatest single contributions to statistical theory" (E. Pearson, 1938, p. 29) and "perhaps Karl Pearson's greatest single discovery" (Mahalanobis, 1938, p. 270).

In his 1895 paper on "Skewed Variation," Pearson had developed a set of theoretical types of frequency curves. The next problem was to find a method of testing a set of observations to see how closely they fit a theoretical curve, whether it was a normal curve or one of Pearson's other theoretical types. Pearson suspected as early as 1894 that some of the data used by textbook authors to illustrate the normal curve really did not fit the normal curve very well. In this paper, he devised a general method for testing the fit of any set of data to any curve.

The chi-square paper is a difficult one; even Gosset once wrote that he had only understood about one-third of it (E. Pearson, 1939, p. 390). The paper begins not with a discussion of a practical problem but with a theoretical presentation of the derivation of the chi-square formula. The first six pages are mostly algebraic symbols, but on the seventh page Pearson presents the following formula:

$$\chi = \sqrt{\,} S(\frac{e^2}{m})$$

This formula is for χ rather than χ^2. If both sides of the equation are squared, we have the following formula:

$$\chi^2 = S(\frac{e^2}{m})$$

This is equivalent to the modern formula for chi-square, since S is a sign for summation, e is the difference between an observed frequency and a theoretical frequency, and m is a theoretical frequency. At the end of his article, Pearson included a table for looking up probability levels for particular chi-square values. The rows of the table corresponded to chi-square values, and the columns corresponded to n', or the number of groups plus one. The table does not give the same values for chi-square as our modern tables because the application of chi-square was changed later when Fisher introduced the concept of *degrees of freedom*.

Pearson gave in his paper examples of the application of the chi-square test to eight different sets of data. First, he tested

26,306 throws of 12 dice to see if the dice were biased. The observed frequencies for the dice throws came from Weldon, who, shared the throwing duties with his wife. Table 4.2 presents the number of dice in each cast with either 5 or 6 points showing. From the binomial theorem, it is possible to calculate the theoretical frequencies with which each count should occur.

The table shows 5 and 6 points occurring more frequently than they should occur according to theory. But are the deviations so great that it is unreasonable to attribute them to chance? Pearson computed a chi-square value of 43.87241, and a probability of 0.000016 that the results occurred by chance. Therefore, he concluded that the dice were biased in such a way that the higher points were more likely.

Pearson also applied his formula to 4,274 sets of roulette run at Monte Carlo in July 1892. He obtained a chi-square of 172.43 and concluded "the improbability of a series as bad as or worse than this is about $14.5/10^{30}$!" (p. 169). He had examined a table of 1,000 shots fired in target practice which Mansfield Merrioan presented in his textbook on least squares (1884) as fitting the normal curve. Pearson concluded that Merriman's data did not fit the normal curve very well, since deviations from the normal curve as large as his deviations would only occur with a probability of 0.00000155.

Edgeworth, whose questions had originally interested Pearson in skewed curves, wrote to Pearson in 1900 about the new chi-square test: "I have to thank you for your splendid method of testing my mathematical curves of frequency. That χ^2 of yours is one of the most beautiful of the instruments which you have added to the Calculus" (Kendall, 1968b, p. 262). Fisher also wrote that chi-square "is the great contribution to statistical methods by which the unsurpassed energy of Prof. Pearson's work will be remembered" (1925c, p. 22).

As time has passed, the original purpose of the chi-square test has almost been forgotten. Instead of being used to fit curves, the test is used much more now as a method of testing hypotheses involving frequency count data. It has become a major tool in sociology and related fields. In fact, some authors have suggested recently (Duggan and Dean, 1968) that too much reliance is being placed on chi-square. The problem is that chi-square works well as a test of the independence of two variables, but it tells us nothing of the strength of association between the two variables.

A recommended procedure for dealing with this problem is to calculate a measure of the degree of association (such as Goodman and Kruskal's gamma) along with the chi-square test.

The Nature-Nurture Controversy

Pearson attempted to resolve conclusively the nature-nurture dispute in a paper in 1903. The article, "On the Inheritance of the Mental and Moral Characters in Man, and its comparison with the Inheritance of the Physical Characteristics," was a direct continuation of Galton's work trying to uncover the laws of heredity. Galton had used his correlation coefficient to show that heredity was at work in the transmission of physical characteristics, such as height. But he had not done a similar kind of research involving moral or mental characteristics.

In this paper, Pearson compared siblings on physical characteristics such as eye color, hair color, head length, and head breadth as well as on mental characteristics such as introspection, assertiveness, conscientiousness, and general intelligence. The latter traits were judged by teachers filling out questionnaires. Some of these characteristics were judged on the basis of two categories, such as "shy" and "assertive" for assertiveness. Pearson computed the correlation between sibling and sibling on each of these traits. In order to find a correlation between a characteristic measured on two categories (essentially what we would call today a 2-by-2 table), he used his *tetrachoric coefficient of correlation*. The data for one of these correlations (the one involving assertiveness) appears in Table 4.3.

In all cases, whether the characteristics being measured were physical or mental, Pearson found correlations of around .5. Pearson wrote, "We are forced absolutely to the conclusion that the degree of resemblance of the physical and mental characteristics in children is one and the same" (Pearson, p. 203). Furthermore, Pearson argued that the coefficient for eye color was about .5, just like all the others, and that eye color could not be influenced by environment. He then concluded that the influence of environment must be small in comparison with the influence of heredity.

Unfortunately, the nature-nurture controversy was not to be settled so easily. Stouffer wrote on this work by Pearson: "His overweening faith in his correlation coefficients as demonstrating the unimportance of the environment as compared with heredity has a quaint, antiquarian ring" (1958, p. 26).

The Founding of Biometrika

Meanwhile, the statistical approach to the study of biology was neither going unnoticed nor unopposed by more traditional biologists. Pearson was working in the summer of 1899 on a paper about the *theory of homotyposis*, the quantitative degree of resemblance between parts of organisms. The paper was based on a huge amount of data gathered by friends and colleagues, and included such things as counts of the veins on twenty-six leaves from each of 100 beech trees. Pearson submitted it to the Royal Society in October 1900, and the controversy began. The Society chose William Bateson, a known follower of Mendel's approach to heredity and critic of the statistical approach, to referee the paper, and then took the unprecedented step of distributing Bateson's critique to members before Pearson's paper was published and before he knew whether it was accepted or rejected (E. Pearson, 1938). Bateson wrote that Pearson's work might be more fitly described as "Mathematical Contributions to a Theory of Normality" instead of "Mathematical Contributions to the Theory of Evolution" (Bateson, 1901, p. 203). At about the same time, the Society passed a resolution stating that papers that applied mathematics to biology would no longer be accepted.

This treatment by the Royal Society led Weldon to suggest the formation of a new journal in which biometric papers could be published. He wrote Pearson on November 16, 1900, that "the contention 'that numbers mean nothing and do not exist in Nature' is a very serious thing, which will have to be fought" (K. Pearson, 1906, p. 302). In the same letter, he asked, "Do you think it would be too hopelessly expensive to start a journal of some kind?" (ibid). This was the start of *Biometrika*, an internationally famous journal of statistics still published today. Galton contributed 200 pounds for starting the journal, and wrote a short article for its first issue, which appeared in October 1901. Pearson thought of the name of the journal, including the "k" instead of a "c" (Pearson, 1930a, p. 241). It was "edited in consultation with Francis Galton by W. F. R. Weldon, Karl Pearson, and C. B. Davenport." The latter was an American zoologist educated at Harvard who might have been included because of his fund-raising ability. Davenport obtained support from the Carnegie Institution for the Station for Experimental Evolution at Cold Spring Harbor, New York, and directed its Department of Genetics from 1904 to 1934.

He became an advocate of Mendelism, however, which may account for his dismissal as editor of *Biometrika* by 1908.[7]

An editorial in the first issue of *Biometrika* argued that "every idea of Darwin – variation, natural selection, sexual selection, inheritance, prepotency, reversion – seems at once to fit itself to mathematical definition and to demand statistical analysis." Galton stated in his article that "the primary objective of Biometry is to afford material that shall be exact enough for the discovery of incipient changes in evolution which are too small to be otherwise apparent" (1901, p. 9).

The clashes between the biometricians and Bateson were not over, however. Bateson walked into the Cambridge meeting of the British Association for the Advancement of Science in 1904 with a package containing all issues of *Biometrika* up to then, threw them down on the table, and said, "I hold that the whole of that is worthless." Weldon, who was sitting beside Pearson, remarked, "At least, we have got his subscription" (E. Pearson, 1966, p. 456). Actually they had not, since Bateson had obtained the issues from the library of the Cambridge Philosophical Society.

Pearson never became a member of the Royal Statistical Society, even though he was the leading statistician of his time. It seems quite likely that his experience with the Royal Society soured him on scientific societies.

Friends and Enemies

In July 1905, Pearson first met W. S. Gosset, a brewer with Arthur Guinness Son and Co. Ltd., in Dublin. Gosset was having problems analyzing data from the brewery, and so he consulted Pearson while in England by riding a bicycle from Watlington to a farm at East Ilsley in Berkshire where Pearson was vacationing. The following year, Gosset arrived at the Biometric Laboratory in London for nearly a year of study with Pearson. Gosset later said he learned more from Pearson's daily "rounds" than he did from his lectures. He said Pearson would frequently come around at five o'clock with tea and seed cake or petit-beurre biscuits and talk until 6:30. Gosset gave Pearson credit for supplying a missing link in the famous "Probable Error of a Mean" paper that introduced the *t*-test (E. Pearson, 1938).

Pearson's colleague and friend Weldon died of pneumonia in 1906, and the death of the younger man was a great blow. The period of fruitful productivity of biometric papers was coming to a close, although Pearson continued to write theoretical papers on statistics, edit journals, draw up some of the basic statistical tables, and inspire brilliant students for the next thirty years. One of the major projects remaining was the mammoth four-volume biography of Galton.

Pearson became embroiled in a number of controversies in the latter half of his life, many of them with younger statisticians presenting new ideas. He disagreed with Gosset over the appropriateness of using statistics with small samples, something Gosset was forced to do because of the nature of brewery work. Gosset had justified this use theoretically, but Pearson never saw the legitimacy of his methods.

Beginning in 1905, Pearson openly disagreed with his former student Yule over measures of association for nominal variables in a 2-by-2 table. Both had developed measures of association for this kind of data in papers published in 1900. Yule's was a rather simple measure of association called Q. Ironically, his paper introducing Q was presented to the Royal Society by Pearson. Pearson's measure was a more complicated one based on the *bivariate normal distribution* (Pearson, 1901), and he termed it the *tetrachoric coefficient of correlation* (the name reflecting the four cells in a 2-by-2 table). MacKenzie (1978) has suggested that the dispute arose because of the different interests of the two men, and particularly because Pearson was committed to eugenics and Yule was not. Pearson wanted to be able to compare correlation coefficients based on nominal variables such as eye color with correlation coefficients based on interval-level variables such as height. To do this, he tried to base both types of coefficients on the same foundation – the bivariate normal distribution. This was necessary for the testing of the power of nature over nurture, as Pearson attempted to do in the 1903 paper described earlier. Yule, on the other hand, was doing research on pauperism that brought out the important role played by environmental factors.

Pearson also had a number of disagreements with Ronald Fisher. Although he had published one of Fisher's first papers in *Biometrika*, the two clashed after Pearson rejected two other papers. Their feud grew to grand proportions toward the end of Pearson's life, with exchanges in print of vicious comments. Part of the problem was that the switch from large sample theory to the small sample theory being developed by Gosset and Fisher required a shift in thinking much like one of Thomas Kuhn's "paradigm shifts" (1962), and this was not easy for Pearson to achieve. He was nineteen years older than Gosset and thirty-three years older than Fisher. Kuhn points out that the people who invent new paradigms almost always are very young or very new to the field. Egon Pearson has commented about his father, "But where perhaps he was at fault was in a failure to recognize that a younger generation was as genuinely chasing along new lines of thought as he had been himself in the '90's. The old watch-dog should have let them pass!" (1938, p. 102).

Pearson also argued with the American anthropologist Franz Boas over who first discovered certain formulas for the correlation coefficient. Boas triggered the incident in 1909 when he published three formulas for the correlation coefficient in Science but did not mention Pearson. Pearson responded with a letter to the editor (1909) pointing out that all three had been used or considered earlier in work by Pearson and his associates, some of which was published in 1896.

Boas had apparently been working with correlation for some time, however. William Bryan (1892) used a type of correlation in his 1892 paper "On the Development of Voluntary Motor Ability" and said he acquired the method from Boas. Guilford (1936) said Bryan's paper was the first application of correlation to a psychological problem. One interesting possibility is that Boas might have learned of correlation from James McKeen Cattell, who had studied with Galton. Boas joined the faculty of Columbia University in 1896. Cattell was already there as head of the Psychology Department and would soon become head of anthropology. Prior to that, both men had been associated with Science magazine.

Boas and Pearson could not have had more opposite views on questions of race and human ability, and it is a wonder they did not come into public disagreement on more important issues than giving proper credit for the correlation coefficient. Unlike Galton and Pearson, Boas felt that all races of humanity had an equal capacity for development. One of Boas's studies of the transmission of heredity from parent to child offered very different conclusions from Galton's and Pearson's correlation studies. Boas took measurements from immigrants and their children, and found that children do not necessarily reproduce the cranial and other features of their parents if they grow up in a different environment

(Boas 1912). Boas was a German-born Jew who had received his Ph.D. at the University of Kiel. Because of his views on race, Boas had his degree rescinded by the Nazis in the 1930s. One author maintains that "it is possible that Boas did more to combat race prejudice than any other person in history" (Gossett, 1963, p. 418). In 1911, Galton died and his will established the Galton Professorship of Eugenics at University College London, a chair which was first held by Pearson. Pearson continued to pay regard to Galton throughout his life. In 1920, the Biometric Laboratory held its first Galton Dinner, a tribute repeated annually as long as Pearson was director of the lab.

Pearson never abandoned eugenics, the program of improving the human race through selective breeding which had been founded by Galton, and, as we have seen, he took it to more extreme positions. Stouffer wrote that Pearson's *Social Problems: Their Treatment, Past, Present and Future*, published in 1912, contains "an exposition of racial and eugenical doctrines which could hardly be more repellent to the contemporary sociologist" (Stouffer, 1958, p. 26). One of Pearson's last efforts in this direction was the founding in 1925 of *The Annals of Eugenics*, which he edited for its first five volumes. Pearson and the eugenics movement eventually drew some strong critiques, including one by novelist and social critic G. K. Chesterton. "There is no reason to suppose that Dr. Karl Pearson is any better judge of a bridegroom than the bridegroom is of a bride," wrote Chesterton (1927, pp. 50-51). The eugenics movement in Britain came into serious decline in the 1930s when the Nazis began adopting such measures as involuntary sterilization.

Pearson retired from the Galton chair in 1933 to become professor emeritus and, ironically, saw the chair filled by his old adversary, Ronald Fisher. They had their most bitter exchange in 1936 over Pearson's use of the method of moments for curve fitting. Pearson died the same year.

Table 4.1
Correlations Between Total Carapace Length and Post-Spinous Length for Shrimp from Five Areas

	r	n
Plymouth	.81	(1000)
Southport	.85	(800)
Roscoff	.80	(500)
Sheerness	.85	(380)
Helder	.83	(300)

Source: Weldon (1 92), Proceedings of the Royal Society of London 51:9.

Table 4.2
Observed Frequencies and Theoretical Frequencies for Getting a "5" or a "6" when 12 Dice are Tossed 26,306

No. of Dice in Cast with 5 or 6 points	Observed Frequency	Theoretical Frequency	Deviation
0	185	203	−18
1	1149	1217	−68
2	3265	3345	−80
3	5475	5576	−101
4	6114	6273	−159
5	5194	5018	+176
6	3067	2927	+140
7	1331	1254	+77
8	403	392	+11
9	105	87	+18
10	14	13	+1
11	4	1	+3
12	0	0	0

Source: Pearson (1900), The London, Edinburgh and Dublin Philosophical Magazine and Journal of Science, 5th series, 50:167.

Table 4.3
Two-by-Two Table Showing the Relationship Between Assertiveness of
First Brother and Assertiveness of Second Brother

First Brother

Second Brother	shy	assertive	totals
shy	679	247	926
assertive	247	399	646
	926	646	1572

Tetrachronic coefficient of correlation = .53

Source: Pearson (1903), *Journal of the Anthropological Institute*, 33:231.

5
W. S. Gosset and the t-Test

William Sealy Gosset, the statistician known as "Student," worked all of his life as a brewer and researcher for Arthur Guinness Sons & Co., Ltd., of Dublin. He was a devoted employee, and much of his life and work can be seen as flowing directly from this commitment. Most of his original contributions to statistical research grew directly out of daily problems of brewing beer or the related problems of growing barley, an essential ingredient of beer. Gosset's use of a pseudonym is another sign of his devotion. While most other original scientists have been able to publish openly and receive credit for their discoveries, Gosset was happy, or at least willing, to remain anonymous and unacknowledged. It is conceivable that toward the end of his life, when he had achieved a degree of fame, he could have left Guinness, taken a position at a university, and received proper tribute for his discoveries. Instead, he chose to become chief brewer at Guinness's new Park Royal brewery in London. There would be no "Galton Dinners" honoring Gosset.

Francis Galton was a Victorian gentleman scientist and Karl Pearson was a university teacher and scholar. Gosset was still a third type of thinker – a researcher employed by industry and basically motivated toward solving practical research problems arising in industry. Even the few controversies in which Gosset became involved are more comprehensible when we realize that he was often taking the side of the practitioner. In the controversy with Fisher over randomized versus systematic assignment in analysis of variance, Gosset was articulating the position of his friend E. S. Beaven, the practical agriculturalist. And in the very basic dispute with Pearson over small samples, Gosset was always thinking of the practical necessity of taking small samples in brewery work and agricultural research.

In comparison with Galton, Pearson, and Fisher, Gosset wrote only a handful of papers. Yet these papers were just as influential as the larger number of publications by any of the other men, particularly his 1908 article introducing the z distribution. This paper led directly, with only a few modifications, to the t-test. It profoundly influenced the development of analysis of variance and introduced a revolution in thinking that led to a series of other statistical tests.

Gosset led a much more isolated life than the other three major statisticians. Dublin was physically separated from the intellectual activity of Oxford, Cambridge, and London. The Irish Civil War was taking place during part of the time that Gosset lived and worked in Ireland. He had trouble acquiring copies of journals and scholarly papers – a necessity for anyone doing original research — and it was more difficult for him to attend scientific meetings. Gosset didn't even meet Fisher until the two men had been corresponding for ten years. Galton had explored Africa; Pearson made frequent visits to Germany; and Fisher was to travel all over the world teaching statistics. Gosset stayed at home in Ireland, except for occasional trips to England to visit relatives.

Gosset's work has become so essential to modern statistics that it is commonly discussed in articles not even citing his papers. Sometimes there are references to "Student's t-test" or "Student's t-distribution," but often the references are only to the "t-test" or the "t-distribution." The terminology has even evolved to the point that the word "studentized" frequently appears without capitalization or quotation marks. This is surely a great tribute to the man, even if most people using the t-test might not recognize the name of William Sealy Gosset.

Early Years

Gosset was born June 13, 1876, at Canterbury, England, the eldest son of Colonel Frederic Gosset of the Royal Engineers, and Agnes Sealy Gosset. He was descended on his father's side from a family that had left France to escape persecution after the revocation of the Edict of Nantes (Irwin, 1968) – the same reason that Abraham De Moivre had come to England.

Gosset attended Winchester College, a public grammar school founded in conjunction with New College at Oxford. One of his fellow students was G. H. Hardy, later to be recognized as the leading English mathematician of his time. In the introduction to a book by Hardy, C. P. Snow wrote that Winchester was "then and for long afterwards the best mathematical school in England" (Snow, 1967, p. 17). Snow indicates that Winchester at that time, like other Victorian public schools, was a pretty rough place and that Hardy almost died one winter. Hardy later did original research in prime number theory and developed the Hardy-Weinberg law, an important principle in genetics.

Gosset once speculated that Fisher might have studied with Hardy at Cambridge, and put the following postscript in a letter to Fisher:

> I think you were a pupil of G. H. Hardy and often wonder whether he put you on to my problems. I once sent him an offprint with an appeal for help, but though I used to see a lot of him at school and even while we were undergraduates he did not reply: he always did scorn applied Mathematics except cricket averages. (Gosset 1970, Letter 2).

Fisher's reply has not been preserved, so it is not possible to know whether Fisher did study with Hardy.

Hardy had an interesting view of mathematical creation, and it is provocative to think of Gosset and perhaps Fisher being influenced by his thinking. Hardy wrote:

> I believe that mathematical reality lies outside us, that our function is to discover or observe it, and that the theorems which we prove, and which we describe grandiloquently as our "creations," are simply our notes of our observations. This view has been held, in one form or another, by many philosophers of reputation from Plato onwards. (Hardy, 1940, pp. 123-124)

After attending Winchester, Gosset wanted to join the Royal Engineers, like his father. After being rejected by the Woolwich Military Academy because of poor eyesight (McMullen, 1958), Gosset then went to New College, Oxford, where Hardy also continued his studies. Gosset was a Scholar of New College from 1895 to 1899. His major subject was chemistry, but he also took a First Class in Mathematics Moderations (the equivalent of a minor in mathematics).[1]

After graduation, Gosset took a position at the Guinness brewery in Dublin in 1899. Gosset was one of a group of young scientists hired by Guinness in the late 1880s and early 1890s. This step was part of a widespread movement of scientifically trained engineers into industry. Andrew Carnegie is said to have commented on this trend: "The trained mechanic of the past . . . is now to meet a rival in the scientifically educated youth, who will push him hard – very hard indeed" (Kevles, 1978, p. 61). The graduates hired by Guinness had degrees primarily in chemistry and physics; and Gosset was probably the most mathematically qualified of the group.[2]

The Guinness brewery was founded in 1759 by Arthur Guinness. He located the brewery on the southern side of the Liffey River and on the western side of the city near St. James Gate, an entrance gate to the city which has since disappeared. The Guinness company is the largest in Ireland, and its bitter, black stout, sometimes referred to as "the wine of Ireland," is world famous. The company is now also known for publishing the *Guinness Book of World Records,* a book which developed as a means of settling arguments in pubs about the largest, the longest, the hottest, the wettest, and so forth.

When Gosset came to Dublin, James Joyce, the author of *Ulysses* and one of the world's greatest novelists, was attending University College Dublin only a few miles away from the Guinness brewery. In fact, if Joyce's father had had his way, these two very different geniuses might have become coworkers. When Joyce received his Bachelor of Arts degree in 1902, his father urged him to become a clerk at Guinness's brewery. Joyce declined and, at this point, opted for medical school (Ellmann, 1959, p. 101).

The name of "Arthur Guinness, Sons & Company, Ltd." is an underlying rhythmic phrase in Joyce's *Finnegan's Wake.* In one form, it appears as "Awful Grimmest Sunshot Cromwelly, Looted" (Ellman, 1975, p. 321).

The Man Behind the Pseudonym

Gosset was a family man, an avid outdoorsman, an amateur carpenter, and a boat builder. He married Marjory Surtees Philpotts, captain of the English Ladies Hockey team (McMullen, 1958), and they had one son and two daughters. In addition to his brewery work, Gosset invented a boat with two rudders that would be easy to maneuver while fly fishing. The boat was described in the *Field* magazine of March 28, 1936. Gosset's coworker at the brewery, Launce McMullen, wrote that he was on the maiden voyage and "had the honour to be nearly frozen to death" (1939, p. 359).

McMullen added that in his carpentry as well as in statistics, Gosset disliked "complicated or specific tools." He once saw Gosset using a pocket knife to countersink some screw holes, and offered him a countersinking bit, but "he declined it with some embarrassment, as he would not have liked or perhaps could not have explained why he preferred using the pen-knife" (1939, p. 359). McMullen also notes that Gosset frequently made minor arithmetical errors in his computations and did much of his work on the backs of envelopes and other scraps of paper.

Gosset possessed old-fashioned virtues — loyalty, modesty and kindness, plus a twinkling sense of humor. Not only was he loyal to the Guinness Company, but he was also loyal to his friends. He remained devoted to Pearson and Fisher even when he was having public disagreements with them.

Gosset's modesty is indicated not only by his willingness to accept a pseudonym all his life, but also by the self-effacing remarks he occasionally made. A young statistician went to see Gosset in x937 and said to him, "On behalf of fellow statisticians, I would like to thank you for all that you have done for the advancement of statistics." Gosset's reply was, "Oh, that's nothing — Fisher would have discovered it all anyway" (Cunliffe, 1976, p. 4).

On another occasion, Gosset was trying to solve the "chessboard error problem," or the problem of analysis of variance, when he heard that Yule was working on it. "If he is," Gosset said, "he has doubtless got something as good or better, and he can put mine in the W.P.B. [waste paper basket]" (E. Pearson, 1939, p. 388).

Gosset frequently devoted his energy to smoothing over disagreements between his fellow statisticians. When Fisher became upset over a review in Nature of his Statistical Methods for Research Workers by Egon Sharpe Pearson, Gosset even composed drafts of possible replies for Fisher to submit.

The writer of an obituary for Gosset in the Journal of the Royal Statistical Society remembered his first contact with Gosset:

> I well remember the uneasiness with which I studied the figures of some of the earliest small-scale tests [of barley] and the sense of relief when I was invited by a member of Messrs. Guinness' staff to submit my data to a "young member of the brewing staff named Gosset" for statistical examination. The letter I received in reply from Gosset, one of a long series which I still prize, was clear, con-

cise, full of help and promise of future assistance – a key, as I learned in time, to a very sterling character. (H.H., 1938, p. 248)

An old friend also writing an obituary in the *Journal of the Royal Statistical Society* stated:

Did you ever hear Gosset say an unkind thing about anyone? He had an excuse for all the failings of other people, and how he enjoyed life – wet or fine – in bad days or good! It is indeed a tragedy that he should be deprived of life at 61, and his friends of one who made for peace and happiness. (E. M. E., 1938, p. 251)

Brewery Work

The brewing of beer involves four basic ingredients – barley, hops, yeast, and water. Barley is used to make the malt; hops is added for flavor and to help preserve the beer; yeast acts on the malt through fermentation to yield alcohol and carbon dioxide; and water provides the basis for the entire process.

Before Guinness started hiring young scientists from Oxford and Cambridge in the 1890s, brewing was a somewhat mysterious process that probably had not changed much in hundreds of years. Gosset and his colleagues applied the achievements of the scientific revolution to the brewing process by beginning to analyze and control the raw materials in new ways. They utilized scientific instruments to record temperature and other aspects of the brewing process, and introduced careful measurements to the entire process – measurements which naturally required some kind of statistical treatment.

One of the first problems Gosset tackled was how various factors affected the length of time Guinness remained potable (as measured by acidity). Gosset wrote to Fisher, "If you have ever drunk Guinness in England you will understand why" (Gosset, 1970, Letter 2). One of the factors involved was the condition of the malt. But another complicating factor, which also affected acidity and had to be taken into account in the analysis, was the temperature at the time of brewing and during storage.

At this time, the scientific revolution was also beginning to be felt in the field of agriculture. This diffusion of knowledge had an important effect on work at the Guinness brewery. Agricultural researchers like E. S. Beaven were conducting large-scale field experiments to try to produce the best possible barley. An experiment of this type might involve treating the same variety of barley with two types of fertilizers to see which produced the best yield. The measurement and comparison of these yields would also lead naturally to some kind of statistical analysis. Gosset became involved quite early in the analysis of these agricultural experiments.

Both types of experiments – the ones in the brewery and the agricultural field experiments – were limited in the number of trials that could be made. In the brewery, an experiment might take an entire day, and thus it might only be possible to repeat the experiment eight to twelve times. This meant that the brewers were forced to apply statistical concepts to samples much smaller than those generally used by other statisticians. For example, Pearson and Weldon in their biometric work were accustomed to working with sample sizes in the hundreds or thousands.

Gosset first turned for statistical help to already published books – Mansfield Merriman's *A Text-Book on the Method of Least Squares* and Sir George Biddell Airy's *Theory of Observations*. Merriman, an American professor of civil engineering at Lehigh University, wrote for "civil engineers who have not had the benefit of extended mathematical training" (1884, p. iii). Merriman's book had provided the target-shooting data that Pearson had analyzed in his 1900 paper on chi-square and found did not fit the normal curve.

Merriman's book dealt primarily with problems of surveying, such as measuring an angle with a transit. Even the most skilled surveyor would attain slightly different readings in repeated attempts to measure the same angle. Mansfield showed, as had been understood since the time of Simpson, that the mean is the best estimate for the true measurement when a number of measurements vary. He then went on to explain the probable error as an indication of the precision of measurement. The probable error is an error of such a value that any given error is as likely to exceed it as to be less than it. For instance, if an angle was measured with a probable error of 1.35 seconds, than half the measurements taken would be within ±1.35 seconds of the mean. Merriman gave a formula for the probable error of a single observation that is basically analogous to the standard deviation as we know it today. He also formulated the probable error of a mean that is the foundation of the present standard error of a mean.

In surveying, the probable error of the mean was usually very small in comparison with the mean. Angles are measured in degrees, minutes, and seconds. With a good surveyor, the probable error of the mean was often a fraction of a second. This situation was different from what Gosset faced in the brewery, where observations fluctuated wildly and probable errors could be large.

Merriman gave some justification for small sample work, at one point including as an example a probable error computed from eight cases. The great precision of surveying made this an acceptable procedure; Gosset faced a tougher task in trying to deal with small samples of the highly variable materials used in brewing.

Merriman used the symbol t to stand for the ratio of x, the limiting error, to r, the probable error. The *limiting error* is the deviation from the mean beyond which observations will be rejected. This ratio has some similarities to the statistic that Gosset was to invent under the name of x, but that later became known as t. Merriman also presented a table for his t values and their corresponding probability levels. This table is somewhat similar to modern t tables, although his probability levels are based on the normal distribution and not the still undiscovered t distribution. It was based on a table published by Johann Franz Encke, a student of Gauss's, in 1832. Encke's table was in turn based on one published in 1799 by Christian Kramp, the French physicist and mathematician. Kramp had also used the symbol t, and was apparently the first to do so (Walker, 1929). He used it to stand for (in modern notation) $x/\sigma\sqrt{2}$ where x is a single observation. Kramp's t table is also found in Quetelet's *Letters . . . on the Theory of Probabilities*.

Merriman's book introduced some other interesting ideas. He explained the concept of *mean error*, which he said is used in German books. This mean error is identical to the concept Pearson later named the standard deviation. He advocated a concept called the *huge error*, defined as an error of such magnitude that 999 errors out of 1,000 are less than it, and only one is greater, which did not become widely used. Merriman also discussed the probable error of the probable error, showing some thinking along the lines of *sampling distributions*.

Gosset summarized some of his readings about statistics in a 1904 report entitled "The Application of the 'Law of Error' to the work of the Brewery," much of which was a rephrasing of Merriman and Airy. He also discussed some original notions that seem to be preliminary thoughts on the correlation coefficient. And he questioned what *odds* should be accepted as being sufficient to establish a conclusion, saying that a mathematician should perhaps be consulted. A note of March 1905, added to the report, indicated that Gosset planned to meet with Karl Pearson to obtain further help with statistics (E. Pearson, 1939).

The initial meeting between Gosset and Pearson was apparently arranged by Vernon Harcourt, a chemistry don at Oxford who might have had Gosset as a pupil and who undoubtedly knew Weldon, Pearson's closest colleague (ibid.). The historic meeting occurred July 12, 1905, when Gosset bicycled across the Berkshire Downs to the place where Pearson was vacationing. Gosset had sent Pearson some questions in advance which can be summarized as the following: (1) What degree of probability should be treated as sufficient for certainty? (2) How should the estimates of error be adjusted to correct for the use of small samples? (3) How can a relationship between sets of observations be expressed? (4) What books would be helpful? (ibid.).

It is not known exactly how Pearson answered the four questions, but in August 1905, Gosset issued a brewery report describing the correlation coefficient, indicating he had received an answer to the third question (ibid., p. 367). The second question was the one Gosset himself solved a few years later and reported in his paper "The Probable Error of a Mean."

The Guinness company had a generous policy of sending employees on a year of study that would benefit their work. Gosset and Pearson must have gotten along well during their summer visit, because when Gosset's time came to spend a year away, he chose to spend most of it at Pearson's Biometric Laboratory at University College London. Gosset arrived in September 1906, and was given a study and invited to attend Pearson's lectures. It was during this time that Gosset did the basic work that led to his first three papers, all published under the pseudonym "Student": "On the Error of Counting with a Haemacytometer" (1907), "The Probable Error of a Mean" (1908a) and "Probable Error of a Correlation Coefficient" (1908b). Gosset's first three papers appeared in *Biometrika*, the journal founded and edited by Pearson. In fact, more than half of the approximately twenty-two papers that he published appeared there.

Guinness records show that the question of the publication of some of Gosset's work arose in October 1906, and the matter had to be taken to the Board of Directors of Guinness. Gosset apparently suggested on October 6 that the research be published "in the name of Professor Karl Pearson and a Student BA." On October 29, the company decided that the work could be published under the name of "pupil" or "Student." Gosset apparently chose the name "Student."[1]

Guinness officials may have required that Gosset use a pseudonym to obscure the fact that it had hired scientifically trained researchers.[2] A managing director of the company has suggested, however, that the nom de plume was merely a result of the tradition that no Guinness employee make a public statement on any subject, scientific, technical, or otherwise (Beaver, 1960, p. 4).

As if having a pseudonym was not confusing enough, Gosset was known by still another name around the brewery. He was referred to as "The General," apparently for no other reason than that there had once been a general of the same name with the military in Dublin.[3]

Because of Guinness policy, the practice of taking a pseudonym was not confined to Gosset. Two of his disciples in statistical work would later take the pseudonyms "Sophister" and "Mathetes," with each publishing at least one paper of his own. "Sophister" was G. F. E. Story, a brewery worker who spent the academic year of 1927—28 studying with Pearson, as had Gosset before him. "Mathetes" was E. Somerfield, a brewery employee who spent some time working with Fisher at Rothamsted.[4]

In the preface to *Statistical Methods for Research Workers*, Fisher points out that E. Somerfield was Gosset's assistant. Gosset's later papers often acknowledged the assistance of "Mathetes" in computing equations and drawing figures. A paper by "Sophister" in *Biometrika* in 1928 received some criticism in an editor's note, and Gosset rushed to defend him in a note intended for publication but never published (E. Pearson, 1939).

A Guinness employee has reported that the company ban on its workers publishing under their own names was not lifted until shortly before World War II (Cunliffe, 1976). Gosset only used his real name once in a publication or public appearance. That was near the end of his life, on March 26, 1936, when he read a paper before the Industrial and Agricultural Research Section of the Royal Statistical Society.

His first paper ("Student" 1907) dealt with error in the counting of yeast cells, a problem of obvious interest to a brewer. Gosset's papers were generally clearly written, and except for the sections dealing with calculus or other advanced topics, can often be understood to a degree by the non-statistician. His paper on "Mathematics and Agronomy" ("Student" 1926a), for instance, contains an unusually clear and concise summary of what statistics is all about.

The Classic 1908 Paper

Gosset's most influential paper is his second – the 1908 *Biometrika* article "The Probable Error of a Mean," which laid the groundwork for the *t*-test. In the paper, Gosset was attempting to solve the second problem he had posed in his early note to Pearson: How should the estimates of error be adjusted to correct for the use of small samples? Basically, he wanted to extend statistical analysis to small samples — including particularly the samples of eight to twelve that were frequently used in the brewery. As Gosset noted in the paper, "As we decrease the number of experiments, the value of the standard deviation found from the sample of experiments becomes itself subject to an increasing error, until judgments reached in this way become altogether misleading" (p. 2). Gosset absorbed the concept of the standard deviation from Pearson. It served the same purpose as Merriman's probable error, and in fact differed from the probable error only by a constant.

Gosset explained his intent this way: "The aim of the present paper is to determine the point at which we may use the tables of the probability integral in judging of the significance of the mean of a series of experiments, and to furnish alternative tables for use when the number of experiments is too few" (p. 2). The use of the word "significance" is interesting since at this point the concept of significance testing had not even been developed.

The traditional wisdom of statistics in those days stated that if your sample was "sufficiently large," you computed your mean and your probable error (or standard deviation) and then referred to tables based on the normal curve to make probability statements. These are the "tables of the probability integral" referred to by Gosset. If your sample was not "sufficiently large," you were not supposed to apply statistics. Gosset thought that there was a way to apply statistics to small samples also, and he attempted to find it.

Gosset began tackling the problem by considering the standard deviation for small samples. In the brewery research, with the highly variable raw materials that were used, the standard deviations often fluctuated drastically. Even though they varied, Gosset reasoned, they might be distributed in a lawful way. Gosset tried to find the curve that represents the frequency distribution of standard deviations drawn from many samples. This was a radical idea – to look at the frequency distribution not of observations, but of repeated measures taken from different samples – and Gosset was one of the first to take this step. Today we would call this kind of frequency distribution of statistical measures a *sampling distribution*. Gosset succeeded in finding an equation defining the curve for the distribution of s, although he did not give a rigorous proof.

Gosset next showed that there is no correlation between (a) the distance of the mean of a sample from the mean of the population and (b) the standard deviation of a sample with a normal distribution. This was necessary before he could take the next step.

This was to find the sampling distribution for the quantity z, defined as the distance of the mean of a sample from the mean of the population divided by the standard deviation of the sample. This ratio had been used in statistics before as a standard part of many analyses. In fact, it is basically identical to Merriman's x/r, and researchers dating back to Gauss's time had used a similar quantity. Before Gosset, no one had tried to find its sampling distribution. What Gosset perceived was that if you could find this distribution, then you could make exact probability statements regarding this ratio even for small samples of measurements. He succeeded in finding an equation for the distribution of z, which is what we refer to today as the t distribution.

Gosset apparently found the sampling distributions of both s and z through a largely empirical procedure involving sampling experiments. At the Biometric Laboratory, he had measurements available for the heights and left middle fingers of 3,000 criminals. From these, he drew 750 samples of four measurements each. He then found the means, standard deviations, and z's for these samples of four and drew the frequency curves for the distribution of s and z. These curves were then checked against the series of types of curves that had been developed by Pearson and were found to fit certain types. Since Pearson had found the general equations for the curves he described, it was not too difficult for Gosset to arrive at equations that seemed to fit.

One of the variable quantities in the equation for the frequency distribution of z was n, the sample size. This meant that the curve shape would change slightly as sample size changed. This was one of the main differences between the z distribution and the normal distribution. The z distribution was really a family of curves, with slight changes in shape occurring when sample size changed. Gosset's article also provided a table giving probability levels for various z values as the sample size changed.

Gosset's paper suggested several examples of how the z statistic could be applied. Although it did not yet have the name, these were really the first applications of the t-test. One of the examples – later to be included by Fisher in *Statistical Methods for Research Workers* (1925c) – dealt with comparing the effectiveness of two sleep medications on ten subjects. This was the first use of what would be later called a t-test of difference scores (Table 5.1). Gosset found that the probability was about .9985 or the odds were about 666-to-1 that drug 2 was a more effective sleep medication than drug 1.

The t-test of difference scores, which is only one type of t test, later became identified with "Student," leading Gosset to comment:

In some American work the taking of differences seems to be considered the essential point of what they are kind enough to call "Student's Method," but this old artifice must at least date back to Noah, who doubtless had occasion to estimate the comparative appetites of his male and female passengers. ("Student", 1926, p. 126)

The paper contained several other examples of applications, including two dealing with barley growing. One involved a comparison of the yields of head corn and tail corn of barley. Another compared the yields from barley that was kiln-dried and barley that was not. These were undoubtedly closer to the kinds of problems that initially led Gosset to develop the z statistic.

The modern era of statistical thinking is often said to date from Gosset's classic 1908 paper. With one stroke, he: (1) discovered a new statistical distribution; (2) invented a statistical test that became the prototype for a whole series of tests, including analysis of variance; and (3) extended statistical analysis to small samples, a feat Pearson and others thought impossible. The paper also in-

troduced different symbols for the standard deviation of a sample
(s) and the standard deviation of a population (σ), a distinction
that would become increasingly useful in future statistical thinking.

Gosset's paper contained some errors; it has even been characterized as "bumbling" (Hotelling, 1951, p. 37) and as working
"without paying too much regard to the rules" (Welch, 1958,
p. 785). As Welch points out, however, this kind of "tentative
guessing" could be very basic to much mathematical innovation.
One is reminded of Gauss's statement that "I have the results but I
do not yet know how to get it" (Beveridge, 1950, p. 200). At any
rate, within a few years Fisher would clarify these discoveries and
show that Gosset was right by giving a rigorous derivation of the z
distribution.

In his paper, Gosset was building primarily on his knowledge of
Merriman, who had used a ratio basically identical to z but had
not investigated its sampling distribution, and on his study with
Pearson, who had introduced the term *standard deviation* and
described a series of frequency curves. Actually, some of Gosset's
thinking on the z distribution had been anticipated in earlier papers by Edgeworth (1883, 1885), but Gosset was unaware of
Edgeworth's work. A part of Gosset's paper – the derivation of the
sampling distribution of s^2 – had been previously done by the
German astronomer Friedrich Robert Helmert, but Gosset did not
know of this work either (E. Pearson, 1939).

The Pearson statistical group published Gosset's paper on z in
its journal, but then paid little attention to the new statistical distribution. Fisher commented that Gosset's work was greeted with
"weighty apathy" (1939, p. 5), and Cochran has noted that "the t
distribution did not spread like wildfire" (1976, p. 13). The acceptance of Gosset's ideas was so slow that we find him writing
Fisher in 1922, "I am sending you a copy of Student's Tables as
you are the only man that's ever likely to use them!" (Gosset, 1970;
Letter 11).

Egon Pearson has suggested that Pearson might not have given
adequate attention to Gosset's work because the year that Gosset
spent with Pearson was the year immediately after Weldon died.
He also points out that Pearson and Weldon were using statistics
for a different purpose than Gosset. They were trying to find small
differences that might provide evidence of natural selection at

work, and that task required large samples (E. Pearson, 1967). Pearson's attitude toward small sample work was conveyed in a letter to Gosset in 1912 in which he said it made little difference whether the standard deviation was computed by dividing by n or $(n-1)$ since "only naughty brewers take n so small that the difference is not of the order of the probable error!" (E. Pearson, 1939, p. 368).

Gosset's attitude was expressed in a letter to Pearson's son written fourteen years later: "It's no good saying 'Oh these small samples can't prove anything'. Demonstrably small samples *have* proved all sorts of things and it is really a question of defining the amount of dependence that can be placed on their results as accurately as we can" (ibid., p. 396).

Gosset expanded the tables for z in an article in *Biometrika* in 1917. The old table had covered sample sizes from four to ten; the new tables ranged from two to thirty.

In 1908, Gosset also published his third paper which paralleled the probable error of the mean paper except that it dealt with the correlation coefficient. He investigated the sampling distribution of the correlation coefficient and discussed its use with small samples ("Student," 1908b). Fisher gave a rigorous proof in 1915 of the soundness of both of Gosset's 1908 papers.

Gosset and Fisher

Gosset first heard from Fisher in 1912, when Fisher wrote him a letter (E. Pearson, 1968). Fisher was just finishing his last year at Cambridge, and at the suggestion of one of his teachers, the astronomer F. J. M. Stratton, he sent Gosset his first paper, "On an Absolute Criterion for Fitting Frequency Curves" (1912). Stratton had been attempting to apply the law of error to agriculture, and had apparently heard of Gosset's work. Gosset thought he saw an error in Fisher's paper, and wrote him about it, but Fisher wrote him back pointing out an error of Gosset's and enclosing a complex two-page derivation of Gosset's z distribution using n-dimensional space as the method of proof. Gosset forwarded Fisher's letter to Pearson, recommending publication of the proof in *Biometrika* and stating, "Would you mind looking at it for me; I don't feel at home in more than three dimensions even if I could understand it otherwise" (E. Pearson, 1968, p. 406). The proof was not published until 1915, when it was included in Fisher's *Biometrika* article on the correlation coefficient. Fisher confirmed in the obituary he wrote for Gosset that he sent the proof to Gosset "before the War" (1939, p. 5).

Fisher and Gosset became close friends, despite a disagreement toward the end of Gosset's life over randomized versus systematic arrangements in analysis of variance. Fisher's obituary for Gosset is a warm tribute to a friend. It also seems likely that Gosset, who had contacts with agricultural researchers, helped Fisher obtain his job with the Rothamsted Experimental Station in 1919 (E. Pearson, 1968, p. 408).

Fisher visited Gosset in Dublin, and Gosset visited Fisher at Rothamsted. The two maintained a lifelong correspondence, from which many of Gosset's letters and a few of Fisher's letters have been published, along with some comments by Fisher (Gosset, 1970). These letters show that the two men not only collaborated directly on several projects, but that they often read each other's manuscripts and proofs and suggested revisions.

Gosset's letters reveal his wit and warmth, while Fisher's are more dry and businesslike. The following from Gosset, which refers to his assistant, E. Somerfield, is typical of his humor:

> A propos of my taking the Triumphator [calculator] home Somerfield who is always using it has had to borrow from all and sundry. Yesterday I found him with the machine which Noah used when quantity surveying before his voyage. The story goes that he subsequently bartered it for a barrel of porter with the original Guinness. Anyhow he doesn't seem to have been able to keep it dry and Somerfield wasn't strong enough to turn the handle. (Gosset: 1970: Letter 13)

The two men finally met in 1922 after corresponding for ten years. Gosset wrote to Fisher, "I have been wanting to meet you in the flesh for some time and I daresay I could pick up some wrinkles if I were permitted to see your office system" (Gosset, 1970: Letter 9). The meeting occurred when Gosset visited his sister in England and the two of them drove to Rothamsted.

During his visit, Gosset suggested that his assistant, Somerfield, might spend some time working and studying with Fisher at Rothamsted. This was arranged, and Somerfield left on December 1, 1922, to spend approximately three months with Fisher. Although Gosset warned Fisher beforehand that Somerfield probably would not be permitted to publish under his own name (Gosset, 1970: Letter 13), Fisher wasn't completely happy about it. Gosset wrote later, "Somerfield tells me that the Guinness attitude with regard to publication and acknowledgement annoyed you. I am sorry, it has annoyed me in exactly the same way, but I did my best to warn you" (Gosset, 1970: Letter 22).

Gosset was not living a quiet, scholarly life at this time, because of the Irish Civil War. He wrote to Fisher:

> You ask whether we are all right through "the riots." We don't have "riots" here though they do in Belfast. Here it is some unobtrusive individual who throws a bomb at a lorry-load of soldiers in a crowded street. He doesn't often damage the solidiers who are mostly driving h for l [hell for leather] nor do the soldiers often hit him, but there are others. I've never seen one of their performances myself. The rest of the work is done at night and we are none of us free from the fear of it. (Gosset, 1970: Letter 12)

The two men began collaborating in 1922 on a revision of the tables for Gosset's z distribution, and it is this work that produced the t-test as we know it today. Many letters between the two over the next few years dealt with the painstaking work of computing these tables. Apparently Fisher used one method to obtain the figures and Gosset used another, and then they compared results. Along the way, the symbol z was replaced by t, and the formula defining the statistic was changed slightly. Eisenhart (1979) has concluded that the shift from the old z form to the new t form was due to Fisher, but that Gosset chose the letter t for the new form. In his letters, Gosset used t when referring to his own calculations and x when referring to Fisher's.

The first use of the new symbol t to refer to Student's distribution came in a talk Fisher delivered in 1924 to a meeting of the International Congress of Mathematics held in Toronto. However, this paper was not published until 1928.

The new tables developed by Gosset and Fisher were first published in *Metron* in 1925 ("Student," 1925), along with a theoretical paper on the distribution by Fisher (1925a). Fisher's paper introduced the concept of *degrees of freedom* for use with the t-test rather than sample size. The t-test did not receive much publicity, or popularity until Fisher's *Statistical Methods for Research Workers* came out in 1925.

Gosset's Work on Analysis of Variance

Gosset became interested in agricultural as well as industrial research when the maltster E. S. Beaven came to him in 1905 with some data from a barley growing experiment. Beaven was responsible for inventing the "half drill strip" method of planting in agricultural experiments. Two varieties of seed, A and B, are planted in long strips which are put side by side in units of ABBA. The technique was effective in eliminating variation in yield due to soil differences. Using a different approach, Beaven and Gosset designed an experiment in 1912 using eight varieties of barley. The varieties were laid out in a "chessboard" design, which was another means of equalizing the effect of soil differences.

Clearly the analysis of these results was going to be difficult with the *t*-test, which grew out of comparisons of *two* conditions. Gosset and Beaven referred to this as the "chessboard problem," and a number of statisticians, including Gosset, Fisher, and Yule, were trying to solve it. Progress was slowed during the period 1914-1919 because the war forced discontinuation of the chessboard experiments. In 1920, Gosset became responsible for the statistical analysis of Irish Department of Agriculture barley growing experiments at several locations; meanwhile, Fisher was working on similar problems at Rothamsted. Fisher finally solved the problem, and in doing so, invented *analysis of variance*.

Fisher's technique was described in an article with W. A. Mackenzie dealing with the effects of potash and manure on the growth of different varieties of potatoes. The article was received by the *Journal of Agricultural Science* on March 20, 1923, and published in July. Gosset described essentially the same method in the paper "On Testing Varieties of Cereals" read before the Society of Biometricians and Mathematical Statisticians on May 28, 1923, and published in *Biometrika* in December 1923. Fisher receives the credit for inventing analysis of variance because he published first, and because he contributed a key element to Gosset's paper by correcting the divisor from $mn - m - n + 1$ to $mn - m - n$. Egon Pearson has suggested that it was really almost a simultaneous discovery because Gosset had individually conceived the key idea of breaking up a total sum of squares into parts (E. Pearson, 1939).

Later Years
Gosset's last years were spent in writing further papers, taking on greater responsibility with Guinness, and becoming involved in several statistical controversies.

One such controversy involved Gosset, Fisher, Egon Sharpe Pearson, and, eventually, Karl Pearson. *Nature* had published on June 8, 1929 a review of Fisher's *Research Methods for Statistical Workers* by Egon Sharpe Pearson. Apparently feeling that he was being accused of dishonesty, Fisher took offense at the review. Gosset thought that the review was fair and basically favorable, and tried to act as arbitrator. Fisher wrote a letter to the editor which Gosset regarded as intemperate, and Gosset tried to convince him to revise it. At one point, Gosset even went so far as to draft a possible response for Fisher (Gosset, 1970: Letter 102).

Finally, after much writing back and forth, Fisher and Gosset both sent letters to *Nature*. Gosset signed his "Student," and gave as his address "The Galton Laboratory, University College London," since *Nature* required an address and he couldn't put down the brewery. This provoked Karl Pearson, then director of the Galton Laboratory, to enter the fray with the following letter to *Nature*:

> Away on holiday, I see in my copy of *Nature* of July 20, p. 93, a letter on this subject from the distinguished statistician who uses the *nom de plume* of "Student." I regret that from some inadvertency he should have dated his letter from the Galton Laboratory, University College, London, an address to which, however much we may regret it, he has no claim. I feel sure that he will recognize, on fuller consideration, that the task of the director of a laboratory would become impossible if anyone could use its address without first obtaining permission of the director. (K. Pearson, 1929, p. 183)

Gosset and Fisher were in another small tiff the same year when Gosset published in *The Eugenics Review* a review of Robert R. Kuczynski's *The Balance of Births and Deaths: Vol. I. Western and Northern Europe.* Kuczynski predicted in his book that the populations of France and England were doomed to die out because of differences in the birth rate and the death rate. Gosset accused Kuczynski of a "sensational attempt to make our flesh creep" ("Student," 1929b, p. 130). Fisher wrote Gosset that "I cannot think how you contrived to be so unfair" (Gosset, 1970: Letter 106). He included a copy of a letter to the editor calling Gosset's effort "a distinctly hostile review" and praising Kuczynski's work as a "valuable little book" (Fisher, 1929, p. 236). The letter was soon published in *The Eugenics Review*.

In 1931 Gosset published an interesting critique of a major

health experiment conducted in Scotland the year before. The Lanarkshire milk experiment was aimed at determining the effect of raw milk and pasteurized milk on the growth of children. It was a massive effort, using 20,000 school children as subjects and costing 7,500 pounds. The official report on the study concluded that the addition of milk to the diet of children produced an increase in growth both in height and weight, and that there was no difference in the effectiveness of raw and pasteurized milk.

Gosset questioned the validity of the study, primarily because of a flaw in the random assignment of subjects to conditions. Teachers were given the opportunity to transfer students from one group to another if any group had an undue proportion of well-fed or ill-nourished children. This meant that the group receiving milk and the group not receiving milk were not equivalent at the outset. Children assigned to receive milk were found to be significantly shorter and lighter than the others. This was probably due to an unconscious tendency by teachers to help the under-nourished children by moving them into the milk group. Gosset concluded that because of the faulty randomization, the experiment "failed to produce a valid estimate of the advantage of giving milk to children and of the difference between raw and pasteurized milk" ("Student," 1931a, p. 406).

Gosset proposed a much cheaper experiment which would have produced valid results. He suggested using identical twins, and then determining by the toss of a coin which one would receive pasteurized milk and which one would get raw milk (or the comparison could be between milk and no milk). The twins would be matched as closely as two people could be on all kinds of factors, but particularly on heredity, age, and nutritional history. Gosset argued that because of this method's sensitivity, fifty pairs of twins would give more reliable results than the 20,000 subjects used in the actual experiment. This method of using twins is, of course, similar to Galton's procedures some years before when he was distinguishing the effects of heredity and environment.

The same year brought further controversy with Karl Pearson. Pearson, who for twenty-three years had had little to say about Gosset's z test, suddenly decided to attack it in a paper in *Biometrika* (1931a). He criticized the use of the same subject in both conditions of an experiment, and discussed the sleep medication data as an example. Gosset replied to the Pearson criticism in an article in *Biometrika* ("Student," 1931b), but then Pearson answered Gosset's reply. Pearson attacked the basic idea of Gosset's z, which was defined as the quantity obtained by dividing the distance between the mean of a sample and the mean of the population by the standard deviation of the sample, writing: "I have never been able to conceive why testing one character is better than testing three" (K. Pearson, 1931b, p. 410). He also attacked Gosset's recommendation in his Lanarkshire milk experiment paper, stating that he seriously doubted that an experiment using fifty pairs of identical twins would give more reliable results than an experiment with 20,000 general students. It seems clear now that Pearson was wrong in this dispute; matching of the type Gosset was advocating and the use of the same subject in two conditions are now basic principles of experimental design.

Despite these disagreements, Gosset and Pearson remained friends. Gosset continued to write letters to Pearson on statistical matters. At the opening meeting of the Industrial and Agricultural Research section of the Royal Statistical Society in 1933, Gosset discussed the importance of the relationship between the practical man and the professor in a manner that seemed to be a tribute to Pearson ("Student," 1934a). Gosset continued to refer to Pearson in a friendly fashion, and apparently viewed him much like a father.

Venturing away from statistics, Gosset published an investigation of some theoretical matters in genetics in 1934. Here he was following Galton's and Pearson's leads by attempting to apply mathematics to the study of evolution. Fisher, who had written a book and many articles on genetics, must have felt that there was some value in this work by Gosset, for he spent a page and a half discussing it in his obituary for Gosset (Fisher, 1939).

In 1935, Gosset became chief brewer at Park Royal, a new brewery opened in London by Guinness. This appointment indicates the high regard the firm had for him (and he for it), and that he was not viewed as just a statistician. The move to London enabled him to attend meetings of the Royal Statistical Society. Gosset read the paper in which he used his own name before the Industrial and Agricultural Research Section in March of 1936; it was the one time that he made a public appearance or released a publication under his own name instead of the pen name "Student." The paper, "Co-operation in large-scale Experiments," drew a great deal of criticism because it advocated Beaven's half-drill strip method for agricultural experiments.

This paper led to further disagreements in print with Fisher. Barbacki and Fisher took issue with some of Gosset's statements, writing, "This enquiry was carried out to test the truth of the opinion expressed by 'Student' that randomization achieves its object 'usually at the expense of increasing the variability when compared with balanced arrangements' " (1936, p. 193).[7]

Gosset's last paper ("Student," 1937c) was a reply to Barbacki and Fisher. He suggested that what we call today a "bad randomization" was the chief drawback of Fisher's approach. By using a strictly random procedure it would be possible to have all the plots with one type of seed grouped together in one area instead of spread throughout the total area being sown. Gosset argued that "it would be pedantic to continue with an arrangement of plots known beforehand to be likely to lead to a misleading conclusion" ("Student," 1937c, p. 366). Gosset also apparently felt that farmers would find it easier to understand the half-drill strip approach. Gosset, of course, understood the importance of studying random samples, and had discussed it in earlier papers, including the Lanarkshire milk experiment paper (1931) and the general discussion of "Mathematics and Agronomy" (1926). But the question here was not about random samples but whether the assignment of plots to receive varieties of seeds should be randomly determined. Attempting to summarize the controversy, Yates has concluded that the half-drill strip method was likely to be somewhat less accurate than suitable random arrangements using the same plots (1939). Fisher himself apparently had no hard feelings toward Gosset and suggested in his obituary tribute that Gosset was defending the half-drill strip method mainly out of loyalty to colleagues (probably Beaven). Neyman and Pearson (1937) point out that Gosset took several months to prepare his last paper, not so much because he did not have the time but because he did not want to become involved in controversy.

Despite their disagreements, Fisher referred to Gosset after his death as "one of the most original minds in contemporary science" (1939, p. 1), and thus spoke for the entire scientific community in honoring this great man.

Table 5.1
Additional Hours of Sleep Gained by the Use of Two Sleeping Medications

Patient	Drug 1	Drug 2	Difference Drug 1 - Drug 2
1	+.7	+1.9	+1.2
2	−1.6	+.8	+2.4
3	−.2	+1.1	+1.3
4	−1.2	+.1	+1.3
5	−.1	−.1	0
6	+3.4	+4.4	+1.0
7	+3.7	+5.5	+1.8
8	+.8	+1.6	+.8
9	0	+4.6	+4.6
10	+2.0	+3.4	+1.4
mean	+.75	+2.33	+1.58

Source: "Student" (1908a), Biometrika 6:20, with one misprinted value corrected from Fisher (1925c), Statistical Methods for Research Workers, p. 121.

6
Sir Ronald Fisher and the Analysis of Variance

The main building at the Rothamsted Experimental Station is brick covered with ivy and looks like an old school building. In front of the structure is a stone monument, erected in 1893, that commemorates fifty years of continuous agricultural experiments at Rothamsted. This is the building in which Ronald Fisher worked when he developed the *analysis of variance*. A visitor to Rothamsted today who is fortunate enough to arrange a tour might end up standing in the same Broadbalk wheat field that has been under continuous planting since 1843 and that provided some of Fisher's first data analysis problems.

Fisher spent fourteen years working at Rothamsted, writing *Statistical Methods for Research Workers* and doing most of the thinking and problem-solving that constituted *The Design of Experiments*. Fisher benefited from the stimulus of practical research problems at Rothamsted in the same way that Gosset benefited from working at Guinness.

Much of Fisher's statistical work can be seen as an extension, through his great mathematical powers, of earlier efforts by Pearson and Gosset. This work falls in the area of theoretical development of mathematical statistics, one of three areas in which Fisher made major contributions. The other two are experimental design, which Fisher practically invented, and genetics, to which he made substantial contributions. In his highly productive career, Fisher wrote about 300 papers and seven books.

Fisher's work in mathematical statistics began filling in some important gaps that had been revealed by Gosset's paper on the distribution of z (later known as t). Gosset had found the sampling distribution of z, but since his proof was faulty, Fisher derived the correct proof. Beyond that, Gosset's work pointed out that the exact sampling distributions of some other also commonly used statistical measures, such as the correlation coefficient, were not known. This meant that for many of these statistical tests, it was not possible to determine significance levels; that is, one could not say that a certain correlation coefficient was significant at the 0.05 level because the sampling distribution of the correlation coefficient was unknown. Fisher began tackling these tough problems of finding sampling distributions one by one and successfully solving them. Part of his technique was the use of n-dimensional space that Gosset had found so puzzling when Fisher wrote him. The discovery of these exact sampling distributions also involved a heavy use of calculus, at which Fisher excelled.

Fisher made many other important contributions to mathematical statistics, including the invention of analysis of variance and the discriminant function. He also introduced several important terms, including *variance, Latin square* (which he learned from the mathematician Euler), and *statistic* as a term for a quantity computed from the sample (as opposed to a *parameter,* which comes from a population). He may also have coined the term *randomization;* at any rate, he certainly gave it the important position in statistics that it has today.

Fisher's contributions to mathematical statistics were so great that Kendall states that during the period 1920 to 1940, "not to refer to some of his work in any theoretical paper written about this time was almost a mark of retarded development" (1963a, p. 440).

Early Years

Fisher was born February 17, 1890, in East Finchley, a northern suburb of London. He was one of a set of twins, but the other son was stillborn. His father was the fine arts auctioneer George Fisher of the firm Robinson and Fisher.

Like Karl Pearson, Fisher demonstrated his precocity while in a high chair. His daughter, Joan Fisher Box, gives the following account:

> At about age three when he had been set up in his high chair for breakfast, he asked: "What is a half of a half?" His nurse answered that it was a quarter. After a pause, he asked, "And what's a half of a

quarter?" She told him that it was an eighth. There was a longer pause before he asked again, "What's a half of an eighth, Nurse?" When she had given her reply there was a long silence. Finally, Ronnie looked up, a plump pink and white baby face framed with waving red-gold hair, and said slowly, "Then, I suppose that a half of a sixteenth must be a thirty-toof." (Box, 1978, pp. 12-13)

Fisher showed an early interest in scientific matters; before he was six, his mother read to him from an astronomy book (Mahalanobis, 1938). Some of Fisher's followers have suggested that his tendency to use geometric solutions and to show great mathematical intuition might have been related to an early phase of his mathematics training. Fisher had weak eyesight, and while he was studying at Harrow with W. N. Roseveare, he was not allowed to work by artificial light. He took his evening lessons by ear, and without the use of pencil and paper. From this, he may have become used to visualizing complex problems in his mind. Kendall has remarked that he only half believes this, however, because "powers such as Fisher's ability to visualize complicated geometrical relations are born, not made, although they may be strengthened by circumstance" (1963a, p. 439).

Fisher was an undergraduate at Gonville and Caius College, Cambridge, from 1909 to 1912. He then spent an additional year doing graduate work there, studying statistical mechanics and quantum theory with James Jeans and the theory of errors with F. J. M. Stratton (Box, 1978, p. 33). He is said to have attended a statistics lecture by G. Udny Yule. He must also have been exposed to the thinking of the great Cambridge mathematician Arthur Cayley, although Cayley had died in 1895. Cayley had been one of Karl Pearson's examiners in the Smith's Prize competition, and before that, one of Francis Galton's tutors. He played a key role in developing the mathematics of n-dimensional space, the concept that Fisher was able to apply to statistics with such power and fertility. Fisher also became interested in eugenics while he was an undergraduate and participated in the formation of the Cambridge University Eugenics Society (Box, 1978, p. 26). He took the mathematical tripos in 1912, and graduated as a wrangler, as had Pearson before him.

Fisher's first scholarly paper was published while he was still an undergraduate. Entitled "On an Absolute Criterion for Fitting Frequency Curves," it appeared in 1912 in *Messenger of Mathema-*

tics. The paper is a highly theoretical work and cites only two references: T. L. Bennett's *Errors of Observation* and Chauvenet's *Spherical Astronomy*. There is no mention of Karl Pearson, although the subject is related to the problems Pearson addressed in his 1900 paper on chi-square. His reference to a "method of moments" is interesting in light of the fact that Fisher and Pearson's last major confrontation twenty-four years later would be over the method of moments. Fisher wrote in his 1912 paper that "the method of moments is possibly of more value [for curve fitting], though its arbitrary nature is more apparent" (p. 156).

Fisher first contacted Gosset at this time when, at the suggestion of Stratton, he sent him a copy of the "Absolute Criterion" paper. Sometime later, definitely by September 1912, Fisher sent Gosset the derivation of "Student's" distribution through use of n-dimensional space. As we have seen, Gosset forwarded the proof to Pearson, recommending its publication, but it was not published until 1915 as a part of Fisher's paper on the correlation coefficient (E. Pearson, 1968).

It is not clear exactly when Fisher became aware of Pearson's writings on mathematical statistics. Kendall (1963a) has indicated that Fisher used to read *Biometrika* over lunch — either at Cambridge or after taking his first job. According to Mahalanobis (1938), Fisher read Pearson's "Mathematical Contributions to the Theory of Evolution" about the time he graduated from Cambridge. Egon Pearson (1967) said Fisher had studied Pearson's *Philosophical Transactions* papers of the 1890s while still in his early twenties. Kendall has concluded, "Little as he might, in later life, have been inclined to acknowledge the fact, he must have been influenced by Karl Pearson's papers on the mathematics of evolution" (1963a, p. 439).

After leaving Cambridge, Fisher held a number of jobs. He first went to work as a statistician for the Mercantile and General Investment Company in London, where he stayed until 1915. Exempted from service in World War I because of his poor eyesight, Fisher held several positions teaching public school from 1915 to 1919. His daughter Joan reports that he was not an effective teacher and hated it. In 1917, he married Ruth Eileen Guinness, reportedly a cousin of the Dublin brewery operators (Box, 1978, p. 46). During this period of searching for the right job for his talents, Fisher continued to publish articles in the areas of statistics and eugenics.

Fisher's Character

Fisher was known for his poor eyesight, the complexity of his thinking and writing, and his temperamental nature. Statistician William G. Cochran has written of once standing with Fisher on the corner of Euston Road and Gower Street in London waiting for a chance to cross the street. Cochran was concerned because traffic was almost continuous and Fisher could barely see. "Finally there was a gap, but clearly not large enough to get us across," he wrote. "Before I could stop him he stepped into the stream, crying over his left shoulder 'Oh, come on, Cochran. A spot of natural selection won't hurt us' " (Cochran, 1967, p. 1462).

Fisher shared the affliction of poor eyesight with two other great mathematical thinkers – Leonard Euler and Henri Poincaré. Euler was blind for the last seventeen years of his life, and his mathematical productivity was said to increase after he lost his vision. Poincaré, the great French mathematician, also had weak vision but was known to have a visual or spatial memory.

Fisher once solved a tough theoretical problem having to do with sampling moments while on a train journey. When he began to write a paper presenting the results, however, he had forgotten how he arrived at the solution. Kendall says the paper "concludes with an obscure section which is no proof at all" (1963a, p. 433). Nevertheless, he still states the paper (Fisher, 1930) is the most remarkable one Fisher ever wrote.

As this anecdote illustrates, much of Fisher's writing can be difficult to understand. Gosset used to joke about the complexity of Fisher's papers, writing to him that "when I come to 'Evidently' I know that means two hours hard work at least before I can see why" (Gosset, 1970: Letter 7). Kendall stated that Fisher had no gift for exposition, and remarked about *Statistical Methods for Research Workers* (1925b): "Somebody once said that no student should attempt to read it unless he had read it before" (Kendall, 1963a, p. r40). Statistician Oscar Kempthorne has observed that in some of his writings "Fisher was talking on a plane barely understandable to the rest of humanity" (1966, p. 13). He frequently omitted the assumptions on which he was working and neglected to cite previous work by other authors.

Many of Fisher's ideas only became popular after they were translated by means of textbooks by other authors. The most notable of these were George W. Snedecor's books (1934, 1937a) for agricultural researchers and E. F. Lindquist's book (1940) for workers in education.

Some of Fisher's most important papers appear in obscure journals, such as the *Journal of the Ministry of Agriculture* or *Proceedings of the International Congress of Mathematics, Toronto.* Fortunately for the scholar, many of his significant papers are available in a volume collated by Fisher himself entitled *Contributions to Mathematical Statistics* (1950). Collecting one's own most important papers before one's death *was* a little unusual, and led to some sarcastic comment by biologist Lancelot Hogben (1957).

Fisher's temperamental nature is evidenced by his disagreements with Gosset, Pearson, and others. His recurring feuds with Pearson have been called "Titanic arguments" (Kendall, 1963a, p. 441) and "titanic battles" (E. Pearson, 1968, p. 416). Joan Fisher Box wrote of her father, "He would 'fly off the handle' for no apparent reason and was fiercely intolerant of petty inconveniences" (Box, 1978, p. 170). She has attributed some of Fisher's lifelong difficulties in personal relationships to his mother's coldness and lack of effective emotional communication.

Despite this kind of reputation, many friends and coworkers have expressed warm memories of Fisher. D. J. Finney, onetime president of the Biometric Society, wrote:

> My own memory of him short-sightedly manipulating complicated algebraic expressions in his microscopic handwriting cannot be dissociated from an equally characteristic picture of him, relaxed and with a tankard of beer poised, declaiming his views on some absorbingly unimportant question to a circle of colleagues at a conference – or from a more personal memory of his silent enjoyment of an opportunity to use one of my wife's best coffee spoons as an instrument for adjusting the burning of his pipe. (1964a, p. 237)

Early Publications

In 1914, Fisher sent to Karl Pearson for publication in *Biometrika* a paper showing the exact sampling distribution of the correlation coefficient. The journal had just published a paper on this topic by Soper, but Fisher's proof was better. This paper was the first published one in which he used the brilliant technique of representing a sample of size n as a point in n-dimensional Euclidian space, a technique that dramatically illustrated his ability to conceptualize problems geometrically. This paper was important because it meant that significance levels could not be attached to correlation coefficients, since their exact sampling distribution was known. At the same time, Fisher was introducing a general method of proof of great power that he would use later to find the exact sampling distribution of numerous other statistics – the mean error, the mean square error, the regression coefficient, the partial correlation coefficient, and the coefficient of multiple correlation. As a bonus, the paper also demonstrated that Gosset's derivation of the t-distribution had been correct. Pearson liked the paper, writing to Fisher, "I congratulate you very heartily on getting out the actual distribution form of r" (E. Pearson, 1968, p. 408).

The paper was published in *Biometrika* in 1915. A quotation from the paper will describe the geometric approach in Fisher's own words:

> The problem of the frequency distribution of the correlation coefficient r derived from a sample of n pairs, taken at random from an infinite population, may be solved, when that population can be represented by a normal surface, with the aid of certain very general conceptions derived from the geometry of n dimensional space (p. 508)

At another point in the paper, Fisher writes, "The five quantities above defined have, in fact, an exceedingly beautiful interpretation in generalized space, which we may now examine" (p. 509). The five quantities were $\Sigma(x)$, $\Sigma(y)$, $\Sigma(x - x)^2$, $\Sigma(y - y)^2$, and $\Sigma(x - x)(y - y)$, in which x and y are paired observations.

Fisher and Pearson seemed to have started well, but their relationship rapidly deteriorated. Part of the problem was that Fisher ran into roadblocks when he submitted his next several papers to *Biometrika*, and so he eventually turned away from that journal, never to publish in it again. The first of these papers was a reply to an article in *Biometrika* by Soper and others (1917) which criticized Fisher's use of the term *inverse probability* in his 1912 paper, although Fisher was not mentioned by name. Feeling that his use of the term had been misunderstood, Fisher tried to clarify it. Pearson wrote back, "Under present printing and financial conditions, I am regretfully compelled to exclude all that I think erroneous on my own judgment, because I cannot afford controversy" (E. Pearson 1968, p. 413). Fisher's second rejected paper was a note criticizing a paper in *Biometrika* by Kristine Smith that dealt with chi-square. The note was rejected by Pearson, revised by Fisher, and rejected again. Pearson wrote:

> Also I fear that I do not agree with your criticism of Dr. Kirstine
> Smith's paper and under present pressure of circumstances must
> keep the little space I have in *Biometrika* free from controversy
> which can only waste what power I have for publishing original
> work. (ibid., p. 416)

Another issue on which Pearson and Fisher disagreed was Mendelism. Fisher wrote Pearson in 1916 that he had completed a
paper analyzing data from humans that were not incompatible
with Mendelism. Sometime during the next two years, he apparently forwarded the paper to Pearson, who had taken a strong
stand against Mendelism in his confrontation with Bateson. In October 1918, Pearson wrote to Fisher, "Many thanks for your
memoir which I hope to find time for. I am afraid I am not a believer in cumulative Mendelian factors as being the solution of the
heredity puzzle" (ibid.).

Still another dispute between the two came up several years later, when Fisher was writing *Statistical Methods for Research
Workers* (1925b). Fisher wanted to include the chi-square table
that had been developed by W. P. Elderton and published in
Biometrika, but Pearson refused permission. Fisher responded by
creating a new form of the chi-square table which is not only more
useful but also more advantageous for Fisher because it was not
protected by copyright. Some of his bad feeling toward Pearson is
suggested by the fact that although he discusses the correlation
coefficient in his book, he does not credit Pearson with its development. He does use some data from a study by Pearson and
Lee to illustrate correlation, however.

Owing to his differences with Pearson, Fisher turned to other
journals and in 1918 his paper "The Correlation between Relatives
on the Supposition of Mendelian Inheritance" was published in
the *Transactions of the Royal Society of Edinburgh*. This paper introduced the term *variance* and laid the groundwork for analysis
of variance. Fisher wrote:

> It is therefore desirable in analyzing the causes of variability to deal
> with the square of the standard deviation as the measure of variabil-
> ity. We shall term this quantity the Variance of the normal popula-
> tion to which it refers, and we may not ascribe to the constituent
> causes fractions or percentages of the total variance which they to-
> gether produce. (1918, p. 399)

Fisher was also at this time publishing nonstatistical papers on eugenics (1914, 1917). He argued, echoing Galton, that "the present distribution of the birthrate is draining the nation of its best ability" (1917, p. 212). The problem, as Fisher perceived it, was that the lower classes were reproducing at a more rapid rate than the upper classes, who were assumed to be more talented. Fisher tried to recommend some means of increasing the birth rate for professional classes and among the "highly skilled artisans."

In a slightly later paper (Fisher, 1922a), also in the *Eugenics Review*, Fisher argued that infanticide served an evolutionary function in that it purged humanity of its most murderous elements. He also issued a warning about modern contraception, saying it would have the unanticipated effect of favoring the reproduction of the people least willing to practice it.

Rothamsted

In 1919, Fisher received two job offers that would take him out of the public school classroom. One was at the Rothamsted Experimental Station located at Harpenden, Hertfordshire, about twenty-five miles north of London. Founded in 1843 by John Bennett Lawes, it is the oldest agricultural research station in the world. In 1842, Lawes had invented a new fertilizer and established the Lawes Chemical Company to produce and sell it. In the following year, he hired J. H. Gilbert, a young chemist, and they began field experiments to test the effects of fertilizers on crop growth. The director at Rothamsted in 1919, Sir John Russell, thought of hiring a mathematician to be sure that the maximum information was being obtained from the lengthy records of yields of wheat and other crops. While searching for a capable mathematician at Oxford and Cambridge, Russell was given Fisher's name by Horace Brown, the Cambridge botanist (Box, 1978, p. 61).

Surprisingly, the other job offer came from Karl Pearson, who wanted Fisher to come to work as a statistician in the Galton Laboratory. Pearson reportedly offered to hire Fisher on the condition that he would approve Fisher's research and teaching beforehand (Box, 1978, p 61).

Fisher chose the Rothamsted job, apparently because it offered greater freedom. He remained there for fourteen years and established it as one of the most important centers in the world for statistical research. Neyman says that Fisher "put his heart and soul" into his work at Rothamsted (1967, p. 1458), and Kendall says that he "flourished in the agricultural environment to a degree which could hardly have been predicted" (1963a, pp. 439-440).

Rothamsted researchers had been analyzing their results mathematically for some time. For instance, Lawes and Gilbert (1880) examined the effects of manure and other fertilizers on mixed grasses grown to produce hay. However, researchers were not sure that they were extracting the maximum possible information.

Workers at Rothamsted were also using experimental design, but it was a rather primitive sort. One of the problems in agricultural experimentation was variation in soil. Researchers had tried to control for soil variation as early as 1849 by scattering repetitions of the same treatment over a field (Cochran, 1976). One agriculturalist, James Johnson, had even taken the complicated step of putting repetitions in the same relation to one another as the move a knight makes in chess. These early experimenters did not know what arrangements might work best, however, or what kind of mathematical analysis could obtain the most information from these experiments.

Analysis of Variance

Fisher's first paper dealing with Rothamsted data was published in 1921. It was entitled "Studies in Crop Variation. I. An Examination of the Yield of Dressed Grain from Broadbalk," and analyzed the wheat yields for thirteen plots in the Broadbalk field over a period of seventy years. In this very first paper, Fisher was in fact applying analysis of variance to the agricultural data, although he does not state that he is introducing a new statistical test.

One of Fisher's purposes in this paper was to examine the widespread notion that repeated applications of fertilizer had "diminishing returns." A plotting of the mean yield over the seventy-year period suggested that three sources of variation were affecting yield: (1) annual variation, coming primarily from weather, (2) steady diminution due to deterioration of the soil, and (3) slow changes other than steady diminution. The third source was unexpected, and was responsible for large changes. Fisher used a very basic type of analysis of variance to assess the contribution of each of these factors to changes in mean yield. He explained the technique this way:

When the variation of any quantity (variate) is produced by the action of two or more independent causes, it is known that the variance produced by all the causes simultaneously in operation is the sum of the values of the variance produced by each cause separately. The variance is defined as the mean square deviation of a variate from its mean, and is therefore the square of its standard deviation. The above property of the variance, by which each independent cause makes its own contribution to the total, enables us to *analyze* the total, and to assign, with more or less of accuracy, the several portions to their appropriate causes, or groups of causes. (pp. 110-111)

The analysis of variance suggested that the slow changes were not due to chance but to some other factor. Fisher looked for possible factors which might have caused the changes and finally selected weeds. Using some detailed records that indicated when weeding was done in the Broadbalk field, he was able to show that periods of heavy weeding preceded some of the periods of maximum yield.

The slow changes due to weeding made it impossible to determine exactly the curves of exhaustion; nevertheless, Fisher was able to advise for certain fertilizers "the need for caution in the application of the principle of diminishing returns" (p. 134).

Fisher also discerned that problems such as the unexpected variation in weeding indicated that long-term experiments might not be the most efficient type. He wrote:

One point of importance which should be emphasized is that average wheat yields, even over long periods, from different fields or for different seasons cannot approach in accuracy the comparison of plots of the same field in the same seasons. (ibid)

Fisher was already realizing the need for better design of the agricultural experiments, and Gosset, after reading Fisher's second paper, concurred. He thought that the Rothamsted workers had done a poor job of devising the experiments and that Fisher should become more involved in their design (Gosset, 1970: letter 29).

In a second paper dealing with Rothamsted data, he presented an analysis of variance much more similar to the type we are used to seeing today. Published in 1923, this was the paper "Studies in Crop Variation. II. The Manurial Response of Different Potato Varieties," which he coauthored with W. A. MacKenzie. The paper dealt with an experimental design in which twelve varieties of potatoes were tested with six types of manure. The experiment had been designed by Mr. T. Eden of Rothamsted in a chessboard pattern. Fisher carried out an "analysis of variation" which allowed him to determine the effects of manure, the effects of potato variety, and the interaction of the two (which appeared in his table as "deviation from summation formula"). He presented the results in a summary table much like the summary analysis of variance tables used today with columns for "degrees of freedom," "sum of squares," "mean square," and "standard deviation." The analysis revealed significant variation due to variety and to manurial treatment but not to an interaction of the two.

The analysis of variance technique depended on determining the ratio of two estimates of variance as a means of measuring how much one variance was greater than the other. Fisher eventually showed that the ratio of two estimates of variance has a known sampling distribution. This meant the analysis of variance could be used for exact tests of significance.

Fisher originally called this distribution the z distribution, and created a table in which one could look up a logarithm of the square root of the variance ratio. The Indian statistician P. C. Mahalanobis and the American statistician George W. Snedecor independently devised a new table in which the ratio itself could be looked up without taking the square root and logarithm first. Snedecor called the ratio the F-ratio, in honor of Fisher, and the terms F-ratio, F-test, and F-distribution are ones widely used today. Fisher himself avoided the use of F, out of respect for Mahalanobis, who had developed the new table first (Box, 1978, p. 325).

Fisher gave the mathematical basis of analysis of variance in his paper "On A Distribution Yielding the Error Functions of Several Well Known Statistics," which was delivered in 1924 to the *International Congress of Mathematics*. The paper showed the fundamental relationships between the chi-square, t, and F distributions (although F was dealt with in the form of the z distribution). The paper also supplied the mathematical framework that was lacking in the 1925 *Statistical Methods for Research Workers*. Unfortunately, the paper was not published and widely available until 1928, and one of the reasons many readers had difficulty with that book was that this mathematical framework had been omitted.

Further Publications

While he worked at Rothamsted, Fisher began publishing widely on a variety of statistical topics. One series of papers dealt with chi-square and involved another controversy with Pearson. Yule and Greenwood had analyzed some statistics on antityphoid and anticholera inoculations using chi-square and another test, and they had found in all cases that chi-square gave what appeared to be too high a probability for a given result happening by random sampling. This discovery led to Yule's (1922) paper which raised some questions about chi-square. In addition, Fisher tackled the problem in several papers (1922b, 1924a), arguing that the problem with Pearson's original chi-square formula was "the inclusion of vacant or nearly vacant classes which contribute little or nothing to the observed chi-square, but increase its expectation" (Fisher, 1925b, p. 22). Fisher added the concept of degrees of freedom to the chi-square test and developed a new form of the chi-square table and the dispute over chi-square became quite spirited. The controversy even spread to Italy, with some Italians claiming in a series of articles that they had "annihilated" the Anglo-Saxon theory of statistics (Neyman, 1967, p. 1458). Most statisticians seem to have agreed that Fisher was right.

In 1923, Fisher wrote a paper defending Gosset, whom he thought was being unfairly neglected. Specifically, Fisher was upset by W. Burnside's (1923) article on errors of observation, which did not mention Gosset's 1908 paper on "The Probable Error of a Mean." Fisher wrote, "Student's work is so fundamental from the theoretical standpoint, and has so direct a bearing on the practical conclusions to be drawn from small samples, that it deserves to be far more widely known than it is at present" (1923, p. 655).

Gosset and Fisher's long collaboration on the revision of the *t*-tables came to fruition in 1925 with the publication of the tables and a theoretical paper in *Metron*. Soon after, Fisher followed Gosset's advice and became more involved in the design of experiments at Rothamsted. The results were reported in two important books, *Statistical Methods for Research Workers* (1925b) and *The Design of Experiments* (1935a). Some of the key ideas to be developed by Fisher were replication, randomization, Latin Squares, and factorial design.

Statistical Methods for Research Workers

Gosset and Somerfield read the proofs for Fisher's *Statistical*

Methods for Research Workers in the fall of 1924. Fisher commented that Gosset "disagrees about randomization and does not altogether understand the rZ transformation but gives very useful general advice, especially about the presentation of tables" (Gosset, 1970). In the preface of the book, Fisher acknowledges the assistance of Gosset and Somerfield, using their real names, and also the aid of Miss W. A. Mackenzie, his own assistant.

The book did much to popularize Student's work, as well as Fisher's analysis of variance. To illustrate the *t*-test, Fisher took the sleep medication data from Gosset's 1908 paper and reanalyzed it, using the revised *t* formula and tables. Gosset had found a probabability of 0.9985, or odds of 666 to 1, that drug 2 was more effective than drug 1. Fisher found a *t* of 4.06 and a significance level of less than 0.01 — exactly the result one would get today using any basic statistics textbook.

The book contained the first use of *Latin Square* and *randomized block*, two basic elements in experimental design. Fisher explained to Gosset that he acquired the term *Latin Square* from Euler, and that he was recommending its substitution for *chessboard*, which he considered "overworked" (Gosset, 1970: unnumbered letter between Letters 58 and 59).

The book also introduces the first use of *statistic* to mean a quantity based on observations from a sample (as opposed to a *parameter*, which would refer to a quantity from a population). Although this idea goes back to Gosset's use in his 1908 paper for *s* for a sample standard deviation and σ for a population standard deviation, no one before Fisher had given it a general name.

Gosset reviewed *Statistical Methods for Research Workers* in *The Eugenics Review* and commented on its difficulty. He wrote, "It should not be expected that full, perhaps even in extreme cases any, use can be made of such a book without contact, either personal or by correspondence with someone familiar with its subject matter" (Student," 1926b, p. 150).

Further Work at Rothamsted

Fisher took the unusual step of disagreeing with his own boss in print in a 1926 article. Sir John Russell had written that agricultural experiments should be simple, but Fisher argued that they should be complex. He presented the idea of *factorial design*, in which several variables are varied at once instead of just one. Fisher wrote:

No aphorism is more frequently repeated in connection with field trials, than that we must ask Nature few questions, or, ideally, one question, at a time. This writer is convinced that this view is wholly mistaken. Nature, he suggests, will best respond to a logically and carefully thought out questionnaire; indeed, if we ask her a single question, she will often refuse to answer until some other topic has been discussed (1926, p. 17.511).

The advantage of the factorial experiment is, of course, that it provides information on the *interaction* of variables that can never be obtained by studying one variable at a time.

The 1926 paper seems to contain the first specific discussion of the concept of significance levels, although the idea of odds against a hypothesis being true had been used by Arbuthnot, Bernoulli, De Moivre, Laplace, and others. Fisher presented the concept this way:

> First, if the experimenter could say that in twenty years experience with uniform treatment the difference in favour of the acre treated with manure had never before touched 10 percent, the evidence would have reached a point which may be called the verge of significance; for it is convenient to draw the line at about the level at which we can say: "Either there is something in the treatment, or a coincidence has occurred such as does not occur more than once in twenty trials." This level, which we may call the 5 percent point, would be indicated, though very roughly, by the greatest chance deviation observed in twenty successive trials. (p. 17.504)

Fisher's recommendations involved some rather drastic changes for conducting agricultural experiments, and the ideas took a while to catch on. Frank Yates, an associate of Fisher's at Rothamsted, has said that the new ideas were accepted readily there, but that their general acceptance ran into more resistance (Yates 1964). For example, many objected to the randomization of assignment of plots to treatments on the grounds that it complicated field operations and was less accurate than well-chosen systematic arrangements. This latter point is the one that led to the disagreement in print between Gosset and Fisher. Neyman has said that Fisher's ideas were accepted with reluctance, with a frequent reaction being, "Oh, get that Fisher out of my hair — I know about experimentation and about my material, all that I need to know!" (Neyman, 1976, p. 165).

"The Design of Experiments"

Although it was not published until 1935, when Fisher had left Rothamsted, *The Design of Experiments* can be seen as the summation of much of his Rothamsted work. Statistician Oscar Kempthorne has said the book "is regarded almost uniformly as a classic" (1966, p. 17).

Fisher begins Chapter 2 with this sentence: "A lady declares that by tasting a cup of tea made with milk she can discriminate whether the milk or the tea infusion was first added to the cup" (1935a, p. 11). He goes on to discuss the famous "lady tasting tea" experiment, a hypothetical research project he uses to highlight many of the important principles of experimental design, including tests of significance, the null hypothesis, sensitivity, and randomization.

Kendall (1963a) says that Fisher told him he never actually tried the experiment. Joan Fisher Box comments, however, that it evolved from an actual incident in her father's life (Box, 1978, p. 134). A number of researchers were having tea at Rothamsted, and Fisher drew a cup of tea from the urn and offered it to B. Muriel Bristol, an algologist (algae scientist). She said she preferred a cup to which milk had been added first. Fisher said, "Nonsense. Surely it makes no difference." William Roach, another researcher, suggested that they arrange a test. Roach claimed that Brostol identified enough cups correctly to prove her point. Although Fisher's verdict was not recorded, he obviously began thinking about the problem and how it could be solved.

The experiment Fisher describes in *The Design of Experiments* involves preparing four cups with the tea added first and four cups with the milk added first, putting the cups in a random order unknown to the lady, and then asking her to identify the four of each type. By examining the probabilities of combinations that apply to the eight cups, Fisher showed that a person with no ability to discriminate would have all eight cups right one out of seventy times. This leads to the concept of *statistical significance*. If the lady identifies all eight cups correctly, she is doing something that would happen by chance only one out of seventy times. Most people would probably agree that this is a low probability for the outcome to have happened by chance and that it must have happened for a reason other than chance; therefore, the lady really could discriminate the types of cups. Fisher says that it is "usual and convenient" for researchers to take one out of twenty, or 0.05, as a standard level of significance (p. 13).

Fisher also formulated the concept of *null hypothesis.* In this example, the null hypothesis is the hypothesis that the judgments given are not influenced by the order in which the ingredients were added. "Every experiment," Fisher wrote, "may be said to exist only in order to give the facts a chance of disproving the null hypothesis" (p. 16). Fisher described several methods of increasing the *sensitivity* of the experiment, or its ability to detect small differences, one of which is simply to increase the number of cups. If twelve cups were used instead of eight, for instance, the odds of getting all correct by chance alone would be one out of 924. The probability of getting ten out of twelve right would be thirty-six out of 924. Adding these two together, the odds would be thirty-seven out of 924, or less than 0.05, that a person would get ten or more right by chance alone. This increases the sensitivity because the subject can get some wrong and still achieve a statistically significant level of success.

Fisher discusses the principle of *randomization* as a means of negating the effects of other variables, such as the thickness and color of the cups. One way of eliminating the influence of these kinds of variables would be to make all the cups exactly alike except for the factors being tested. However, Fisher says that this is "totally impossible" in the tea cup experiment or in any other experiment (p. 18). In the tea tasting experiment, randomization makes it impossible for the subject to get any kind of clue about what is in a given cup from its color, thickness, or similar characteristics. In other types of experiments, such as a psychological one comparing the reactions of two groups of subjects, a random assignment of subjects to groups eliminates the effects of other variables in the situation — it becomes a means of making the two groups equivalent. The principle of randomization has been called "the most basic of Fisher's numerous ideas" (Neyman, 1976, p. 163), "perhaps Fisher's most fundamental contribution" (Campbell and Stanley, 1966, p. 2), and "the central component of his contribution to the practice of scientific experiment" (Finney, 1964b, p. 327).[1]

The Design of Experiments also contains Fisher's interesting reinterpretation of Galton's analysis of some plant growth data reported in Darwin's *The Effects of Cross and Self-Fertilization in* the Vegetable Kingdom (1876). Fisher uses the information mainly to introduce the t-test. Galton's analysis of Darwin's data may have been one of the first attempts at mathematical analysis of an experiment (Cochran, 1976). The Darwin experiment dealt with fifteen pairs of Zea mays plants (a type of corn), with one plant in each pair being self-fertilized and the other being cross-fertilized. The pairs were grown in the same pots, with as many factors held constant as possible, and then the heights were measured to within one eighth of an inch (Table 6.1).

Fisher points out that Galton used an incorrect procedure of rearranging each series of heights — the one for cross-fertilized plants and the one for self-fertilized plants — from the largest to the smallest, and then taking the differences between these rearranged scores. This arrangement had the effect of artificially reducing the variability of the difference scores. Although Galton had been rather cautious about reaching a definite conclusion, he did notice that in his fifteen rearranged pairs, the cross-fertilized plant was larger in thirteen cases. Fisher observed that Galton had apparently failed to notice that this was also true of the pairs before they were rearranged. Fisher's main purpose, however, was to demonstrate how the data could be analyzed correctly using the t-test. He applied a t-test on the differences between heights for pairs before Galton's rearrangement and found the mean difference to be 20 14 .15 eighths of an inch, in favor of the cross-fertilized plants. Fisher computed a t-value of 2.148, which was just significant at the 0.05 level.

Summers in Iowa

Word of Fisher's work had now spread to America, and as a result he was invited to spend part of the summer of 1931 lecturing at Iowa State College, which had a thriving and progressive program in agricultural experimentation. Its agricultural research center on the Ames campus was the American equivalent of Rothamsted and, as early as 1915, courses in statistics or statistical methods had been offered in the mathematics department (Harshbarger, 1976).

Fisher found the summer heat in Ames hard to take during his first visit; while living in a fraternity house he supposedly put his bed sheets in the refrigerator during the day to prepare for the night (Box, 1978, p. 316). Having just published The Genetical Theory of Natural Selection, and seen his Statistical Methods for

Research Workers through its third edition, Fisher discussed these subjects in about half of his lectures (Lush, 1972).

Fisher returned to Iowa State College for another summer visit in 1936, and met George W. Snedecor, a mathematics professor who was involved in agricultural experimentation and who named the F-ratio after Fisher. Two of Snedecor's books, *Calculation and Interpretation of Analysis of Variance and Covariance* (1934) and *Statistical Methods Applied to Experiments in Agriculture and Biology* (1937a), helped to translate and popularize Fisher's ideas for workers in agriculture and other fields. By 1970, his second book had sold more than 100,000 copies. The fields of education and psychology were exposed to Fisher's ideas through *Statistical Analysis in Educational Research* (1940) by E. F. Lindquist, professor of education at the State University of Iowa, in Iowa City.

The Galton Chair

Since Pearson was retiring as Galton Professor of Eugenics at University College in 1933, Fisher was invited to take his place. At the same time, the department of statistics was separated from eugenics and turned over to Egon Sharpe Pearson, Karl Pearson's son. Fisher was not completely happy with the arrangement, however, complaining to Gosset that Egon Pearson was suggesting that he not lecture on statistics (Gosset, 1970, Letter 162).

Concurrently, Fisher also succeeded Pearson as editor of the *Annals of Eugenics*. Joan Fisher Box writes that Fisher was friendly with Pearson while Pearson was there in an emeritus status (1978, p. 260). The two men were still rivals, however, and their sharpest clash was yet to come.

Fisher's propensity to arouse controversy came out at a meeting of the Royal Statistical Society in December 1934. Fisher had presented a paper containing extensive formulas, and A. L. Bowley, the bicycling companion of F. Y. Edgeworth, began mocking it:

> I took it as a week-end problem, and first tried it as an acrostic, but I found that I could not satisfy all the 'lights.' I tried it then as a cross-word puzzle, but I have not the facility of Sir Josiah Stamp for solving such conundrums. Next I took it as an anagram, remembering that Hooke stated his law of elasticity in that form, but when I found that there were only two vowels to eleven consonants, some of which were Greek capitals, I came to the conclusion that it might be Polish or Russian, and therefore best left to Dr. Neyman or Dr. Is-

serlis. Finally, I thought it must be a cypher, and after a great deal of investigation, decided that Professor Fisher had hidden the key in former papers, as is his custom, and I gave it up. (Bowley, 1935, p. 56)

Since he and Fisher had played bridge together in Harpenden, Bowley's criticism was apparently good natured. However, Fisher's reply, which was not presented orally but published later in the society's journal, was a restrained, matter-of-fact rebuttal.

In 1936, Fisher published a paper presenting the first discriminant function. *Discriminant analysis* is a technique for classifying objects into two or more groups on the basis of their measurements on a number of variables. It was first used in certain problems of archaeology such as classifying a skull as either male or female on the basis of careful measurements of the jaw bone. Fisher's classic 1936 article dealt with categorizing three species of iris, and showed that the three could be effectively distinguished on the basis of four measurements from each flower. Since Fisher's time, discriminant analysis has become a widely used technique in such areas as weather prediction, medical research, and educational testing (Lachenbruch, 1975).

The same year saw the publication of the Barbacki and Fisher paper criticizing Gosset's recommendation of the half-drill strip method in agricultural experimentation. The ensuing dispute over randomization versus systematic arrangements went on for years, with others becoming involved besides Gosset and Fisher. At one point, some of the arguments became quite sharp as people criticized one another's scientific ability. Fisher dismissed this as "just some Billingsgate" — a reference to the London fish market known for its salty language (Cochran, 1976, p. 21).

Gosset and Fisher had taken different positions on randomization in their discussions of the Lanarkshire milk experiment with Gosset ("Student," 1931a) criticizing the lack of randomization and Fisher (Fisher and Bartlett, 1931) finding it valid despite this lack. As Cochran (1976) has said, "It would have been tempting to ask Fisher and Student: 'Whose side are you on?'" (p. 23).

In addition to the disagreement with his old friend Gosset, the 1930s brought other clashes involving Fisher. One feud centered around the conflict between Fisher's idea of *fiduciary intervals* and Jerzy Neyman and Egon S. Pearson's concept of *confidence intervals*. On another matter, Fisher and Karl Pearson had a "spectacular dispute" over the method of moments versus the method of maximum likelihood (Neyman, 1976, p. 161). Koshal (1933), an associate of Fisher's, had written a paper criticizing Pearson's method of moments. Pearson's reply, one of the last papers he wrote, begins with the question, "Wasting your time fitting curves by moments, eh?" (1936b, p. 34). He sarcastically referred to the paper as the Koshal-Fisher paper, even though it was written by Koshal alone, and said it contained "serious blunders in the calculations" (p. 35). He also resurrected the old 1915 argument with Fisher over the paper by Kirstine Smith, saying Fisher "seems to have quite misunderstood her purpose" (p. 45).

Fisher's reply (1937) was equally biting. He accused Pearson of falsifying some computation to support his case, and added: "We may marvel at a senior scientist whom, for his years and past work, many in England and America would be glad to honour, rushing in to prove by a single example what no single example could possibly prove" (p. 29, 313). Fisher continued his personal attacks on Pearson in writing even after Pearson's death (Fisher 1950, 1956). Ironically, Kendall (1963a) has pointed out that Fisher had many of the same faults of which he accused Pearson.

Later Years

Fisher remained head of the Galton Laboratory At University College until 1943, when he accepted the Arthur Balfour Chair of Genetics at Cambridge, a post he held until he retired in 1957.

In the 1950s, Fisher became involved in the smoking and cancer controversy, stating that the statistical evidence was too ambiguous to conclude that smoking caused cancer. He found himself on the same side as Joseph Berkson, chief of medical statistics for the Mayo Clinic, a person with whom he usually disagreed on statistical matters. Berkson once jokingly said that the fact that Fisher agreed with him was the only point causing him serious doubt about his position (Brown 1972).

Fisher was concerned that evidence of correlation alone was being interpreted as evidence of causality. He suggested in several articles (1958a, 1958b) that cigarette smoking and cancer of the lungs might both be caused by a common genetic factor, a hypothesis which was also compatible with the known data from twin studies. These studies showed that monozygotic twins (those from one egg) were more likely to be alike in smoking behavior than dizygotic twins (those from two eggs), and that this was true even if the twins had been separated.[2]

Berkson had a slightly different objection to the correlation studies linking cigarette smoking and lung cancer. He argued that cigarette smoking was also linked statistically with a number of other diseases, and that it was unlikely that it could be the cause of all these diseases. During the presentation of this argument at a Brussels conference also attended by Fisher, statistician Nathan Mantel asked Berkson if it were not strange to be using evidence linking smoking to death to refute the association between smoking and lung cancer. "Berkson then thundered back at me," Mantel wrote, that "he didn't care if cigarettes were good for you or bad for you — he just didn't want them labeled as a cause of lung cancer. It seemed to me that he then turned to Fisher for support, but got none" (Mantel, 1976, p. 119). The criticisms of both Fisher and Berkson were weakened considerably in the 1960s when well-controlled, randomized experiments did produce lung cancer in laboratory animals assigned to smoking conditions (Brown, 1972).

Fisher was knighted in 1952 — as Galton had been before him. In March 1959, he took a research position in Adelaide, Australia, where a number of his former students worked. E. A. Cornish, who knew him there, wrote:

> Unhampered by the responsibilities of administrative duties and, in the relative seclusion of Adelaide, sheltered from the irritations of scientific controversy, he could be himself, and the *real* Fisher was manifested in his superior genius, depth of general knowledge, endearing manner, unbounded charm, generosity and intensely loyal friendship. (1964, p. 373)

Fisher died in Australia at the age of seventy, the victim of an embolism following intestinal trouble. Oscar Kempthorne wrote soon afterward of his friend and coworker, "I surmise that his writings will be subjected to reexamination and reevaluation for many decades and centuries, just as in the case for the writing of Francis Bacon, David Hume and Thomas Bayes" (1966, p. 11).

Table 6.1
Charles Darwin's Measurements of the Heights of Cross-Fertilized and Self-Fertilized Plants (Analyzed by Francis Galton and Later by Ronald Fisher)

Cross-Fertilized Plants	Self-Fertilized Plants
$23\frac{1}{2}$	$17\frac{3}{8}$
12	$20\frac{3}{8}$
21	20
22	20
$19\frac{1}{8}$	$18\frac{3}{8}$
$21^{4/8}$	$18\frac{5}{8}$
$22\frac{1}{8}$	$18\frac{5}{8}$
$20\frac{3}{8}$	$15^{2/8}$
$18^{2/8}$	$16^{4/8}$
$21\frac{5}{8}$	18
$23^{2/8}$	$16^{2/8}$
21	18
$22\frac{1}{8}$	$12^{6/8}$
23	$15^{4/8}$
12	18

Source: Fisher (1935a), *The Design of Experiments*, p. 30.

7
Statistical Creativity

The correlation coefficient, chi-square test, t-test, and analysis of variance have become so prevalent and accepted in today's research that many users probably do not realize: (1) that these techniques were invented, discovered, or developed by human beings; and (2) that they were often initially proposed with some tentativeness and without great awareness of the purposes they would eventually come to serve.

We have seen in past chapters the groping process that resulted in some of these techniques and the modesty with which they were frequently presented. None of the four major statisticians — with the possible exception of Pearson — set out with the particular intention of inventing a new statistical test.

Galton was searching for a mathematical expression of the law defining the relationship between the occurrence of certain characteristics in parents and the occurrence of the same characteristics in their children, which he called the "Ancestral Law." He found a formula with the general capability of expressing many different kinds of relationships, and which we refer to today as the correlation coefficient.

Pearson developed chi-square as a method of measuring the fit between a set of observations and a theoretical curve. Despite this initial development as a measure of "goodness of fit," the chi-square test is more widely used today for a purpose which he did not foresee — the measurement of the relationship between two or more variables.

Gosset was attempting to apply statistical analysis to small samples of the type he was forced to use in brewery work, a procedure that the prevailing statistical wisdom said just should not be done. Undoubtedly he thought the technique he invented would be used in the Guinness brewery and nowhere else.

Fisher tried to analyze the effect of a number of sources of variation on yield in agricultural experiments. Neither his 1921 paper on Broadbalk wheat nor his 1923 paper on the effects of manure on potatoes sounded as though they were introducing a new statistical technique.

To a large extent, these men were intent upon solving particular problems in industry, agriculture, or pure science. But they were also grappling with "anomalies," a step that science historian Thomas Kuhn describes as necessary in the birth of new scientific paradigms. Galton, for instance, noticed the anomaly of children of extremely tall parents being shorter than their parents, and this led him to discover regression and correlation. Kuhn also points out the importance of a "crisis" in bringing out a new paradigm. Gosset may have faced such a crisis when he realized he had to analyze small samples at the brewery but that all the statistical methods developed up to that time depended on large samples. Kuhn offers a description of the breakthrough to a new paradigm:

> ... the new paradigm, or a sufficient hint to permit later articulation, emerges all at once, sometimes in the middle of the night, in the mind of a man deeply immersed in crisis. What the nature of that final stage is — how an individual invents (or finds he has invented) a new way of giving order to data now all assembled — must here remain inscrutable and may be permanently so (1962, p. 89).

This description seems to fit Gosset's discovery of his z statistic, the basis of the later t-test, and Galton's "seeing" of a pattern in his table of heights of parents and offspring.

Mathematics and statistics seem to most people to be very formal and logical fields, and perhaps are regarded as having little to do with creativity. But Jacob Bronowski has noticed that the act of creativity in which an original thought is born is the same in science and in art. Bronowski elaborates on this point:

> Mathematics in this sense, pure mathematics, is a form of poetry, which has the same relation to the prose of practical mathematics as poetry has to prose in any other language. This element of poetry, the delight in exploring the medium for its own sake, is an essential ingredient in the creative process (1956, p. 22).

It is not difficult to see some of this delight in exploration in Galton's perusal of the table of heights that led him to the normal correlation surface, or in Fisher's use of n-dimensional space to find the exact sampling distributions of numerous statistics.

Conditions Favoring Creativity

Why did the development of mathematical statistics take place at this particular time and place? How was it that four Englishmen, born within sixty-eight years of each other, invented all four of the common statistical techniques?

In large part, this statistical revolution was brought about by two developments: (1) the field of biometrics, which was attempting to test the theory of evolution by mathematical methods; and (2) the infusion of university graduates with high-powered mathematical training into industry and agriculture.

The first development — biometrics — was due largely to Galton's reading of *Origin of Species* and his subsequent influence on Weldon and Pearson.

The second movement was apparently worldwide. Daniel Kevles (1978) has described the 1890s recruiting of scientists by industry in the United States, and shown that the old Thomas Edison type of inventing through tinkering had just about reached the limit of its effectiveness. In Britain, there was clearly a similar movement of inviting university-trained scientists to work in industry and agriculture, as illustrated by the hiring of Gosset at Guinness and Fisher at Rothamsted.

Both of these developments drew heavily upon the superior mathematical training available at Cambridge and Oxford — particularly at Cambridge. Cambridge had embodied a tradition of excellence in mathematics going back to Newton and had instituted the rigorous competitive tripos exam to unforce high standards. Brilliant young students were able to study with or be influenced by some of the greatest mathematicians in the world, including Arthur Cayley, James Clerk Maxwell, John Couch Adams, and G. H. Hardy.

Examination of some of the background characteristics of the four major statisticians suggests some additional factors that influenced their creativity besides their university training (Table 7.1). One characteristic that does not seem related to their inventiveness is age at the time of the major contribution, which ranged from thirty-one to sixty-six.

One factor which might have been a strong influence on their creativity was the situation of working together in groups with other scientists. Mathematician S. M. Ulam, the coinventor of the hydrogen bomb, has described the critical mass of a group of scientists working together that "produces results explosively" (1976, p. 293). This factor would seem to apply well to Pearson at the Galton Laboratory and Fisher at Rothamsted. It applies less well to Gosset although he was surrounded by other scientists at Guinness, had statistical assistants, and corresponded regularly with Fisher. It does not apply very well at all to Galton, who essentially worked in the "great man alone" style of his cousin, Charles Darwin.

These thinkers also obtained some of the benefits of group interaction through their extensive communication. Certainly the fact that Pearson, Gosset, and Fisher were frequently in touch with one another, both by mail and through visits, helped to supply additional stimulation and cross-fertilization.

Another significant factor might be that three of the four statisticians were working in the vicinity of London, a highly stimulating intellectual environment — both then and now. Deutsch, Platt, and Senghass (1971) have pointed out that more than half of the major English contributions to the social sciences since 1900 originated in London.

Discovery or Invention?

It is difficult to say whether the major innovations in mathematical statistics have been *discovered* or *invented*. In fact, the choice of which of these two terms to use is an unresolved issue in the field of mathematics. Mathematicians such as George Polya (1973) and S. M. Ulam (1976) use the terms almost interchangeably, as has been done in this book up to this point. Jacques Hadamard, in his book on the psychology of mathematical invention, argues that the distinction between the two terms is almost impossible to make. He maintains that Benjamin Franklin's invention of the lightning rod is hardly any different from his discovery of the electrical nature of thunder. He writes, "Psychological conditions are quite the same for both cases" (1945, p. xi). Hadamard proceeds, however, to state that the nature of invention is different in the field of science and in the arts. The mathematical inventor does not enjoy the complete freedom of the artistic creator. He quotes a teacher who told him, "We are rather servants than masters in

Mathematics" (1945, p. xii). Thomas Kuhn agrees with Hadamard on the impossibility of separating the processes of invention and discovery in science. He wrote, "That distinction between discovery and invention or between fact and theory will, however, immediately prove to be exceedingly artificial" (1962, p. 52).

Ultimately, the question of whether statistical formulas are invented or discovered becomes a philosophical one. It is the question of the nature of the reality of mathematics. We have already seen that the noted mathematician G. H. Hardy believed that mathematical reality did exist, and that mathematicians merely observed this reality and took notes on it. This view can be related, as Hardy noted, to the philosophical ideas of Plato. A contrasting point of view has been presented by mathematician S. M. Ulam: "Mathematics creates new objects of thought — one could call it a meta-reality — by engendering ideas which begin to live their own life in an independent development" (1976, p. 289). Ulam reveals that he is less than certain about this position, however, at another point, where he is pondering the mysteries of n-dimensional space: ". . . . are these marvels of the nature of the human brain? Or is it the nature of physical reality which reveals it to us?" (ibid, p. 279).

Apparently the question of whether mathematical and statistical ideas are invented or discovered hinges on some deep philosophical problems dealing with the nature of reality and our knowledge of reality, and some of these problems remain unsolved.

Contact Between Statisticians

As we have seen, statistics has been a highly interactive field, with most researchers being influenced by and expanding upon the ideas of others. Figure 7.1 is a diagram of the known contact between various statisticians, ranging from the time of Graunt, Arbuthnot, Pascal, and Fermat to the time of Snedecor.

Figure 7.1 suggests that Laplace and Pearson are pivotal figures, with seven lines of influence — more than for any other statistician — converging on each of them. These men were not only able to finish the work of others (as Laplace did for De Moivre, Pascal, and Fermat and Pearson did for Galton and Weldon), but they were also able to inspire brilliant work in newcomers (as Laplace did for Quetelet and Pearson did for Gosset and Yule).

The Figure also suggests that Gosset's work on the

t-distribution could almost have been done in Encke's time, if anyone had been interested in small samples. Merriman served as a middleman in transmitting Encke's and Kramp's work on the probability integral to Gosset, but Merriman did not add much of his own thinking. The only missing ingredient would have been Pearson's collection of frequency curves, which helped Gosset find the sampling distribution for t.

Finally, the Figure shows an intensification of activity from about 1880 on, perhaps indicating the achievement of the "critical mass" described by Ulam.

One Final Myth

One of the tasks accomplished by this book might be the dispelling of a common myth — the idea that the social sciences have borrowed their research methods from the physical sciences.

Galton and Pearson were attempting to find the laws of heredity and were dealing to a large extent with measurements from human beings when they developed the correlation coefficient and the chi-square test. The methods of the physical sciences would not work for their purposes, which is why Pearson was so excited when he came across Galton's concept of correlation.

The research of Gosset and Fisher appears at first glance to fall in the areas of chemistry and biology, but they were much more influenced by Pearson's work and by the field of mathematics than they were by traditional research methods in these two fields.

The social sciences, particularly in the work of Galton and Pearson, have not simply taken over the methods of the physical sciences, but have originated their own techniques.

Statistics Continues

Statistics has come a long way since 1834, when the members of the Royal Statistical Society were reluctant to become involved in data interpretation and chose as their motto "Aliis exterendum," meaning "Let others thrash it out" (Cochran, 1976, p. 8). Most of the statistical tests we had discussed can be seen as attempts to develop more powerful methods of "thrashing out" the meaning of statistical data.

The development of mathematical statistics did not stop with four men who have been the focus of this book. Such European statisticians as Egon Sharpe Pearson, Jerzy Neyman, Maurice

Kendall, Frank Yates, and M. S. Bartlett have gone on to make further contributions. Another phase of this continued development took place in the United States, where Sewall Wright originated the concept of path coefficients; Quinn McNemar, William Cochran, and others developed nonparametric statistical tests; and John Tukey invented his methods of exploratory data analysis.

In fact, the American experience seems to have replicated in miniature some of the English struggles over the emergence of this new field. Mathematical statisticians, who looked upon them as "quacks," and by statisticians, who did not want their journals cluttered up with a lot of "meaningless symbols" (Craig, 1960, p. 835). One can imagine vigorous debates and lengthy controversies of the type that characterized the growth of statistics in England.

Indeed, it is difficult to see how statistics can be labeled as dull or inanimate. After peering beneath the surface of this practical and powerful discipline, we can see that it has succeeded more than once in eliciting strong passions and lively debate among people. And statistics being a product of the human mind, it will doubtless continue to do so.

Table 7.1
Summary of Basic Facts About Galton, Pearson, Gosset, and Fisher

	Sir Francis Galton	Karl Pearson	W. S. Gosset ("Student")	Sir Ronald Fisher
1. Birthplace	Sparkbrook, Birmingham, England	London	Canterbury, England	East Finchley, a suburb
2. Father's Occupation	Banker	Lawyer	Army Officer	Auctioneer
3. University	Trinity College, Cambridge	King's College, Cambridge	New College, Oxford	Gonville and Caius College, Cambridge
4. Degree	Poll Degree	Third Wrangler, mathematical tripos	Major subject, chemistry; minor subject, mathematics	High Wrangler, mathematical tripos
5. Profession	Independently wealthy gentleman scientist	University professor	Brewery researcher	Agricultural researcher, University professor
6. Major statistical contribution	Correlation	Chi-square	t-test	Analysis of variance
7. Specific problem leading to statistical innovation	Finding a mathematical expression for the laws of heredity	Testing the closeness of fit of observations to theoretical curves	Analyzing brewery experiments with small numbers of observations	Analyzing the sources of variation affecting yields in agricultural experiments
8. Age at time major statistical innovation	66	43	32	31
9. Lifetime publications	183 works, including 9 books	500 works, including 9 books	22 papers	300 works, including 7 books

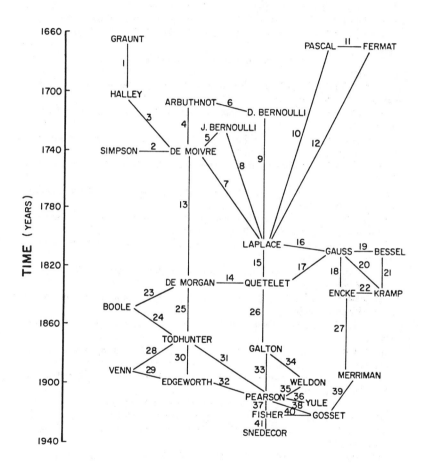

Figure 7.1

The diagram is based on the following known instances of contact:

1. Graunt–Halley. Halley cites Graunt in his *Philosophical Transactions* article on mortality.

2. Simpson–De Moivre. Simpson and De Moivre both wrote on annuities and chance, and criticized each other's work in print (Clarke, 1929).

3. Halley–De Moivre. De Moivre and Halley were friends (Walker, 1934).

4. Arbuthnot–De Moivre. De Moivre cites Arbuthnot in his "Approximation" paper.

5. J. Bernoulli–De Moivre. De Moivre cites Jacob Bernoulli in his "Approximation" paper.

6. Arbuthnot–D. Bernoulli. Dan el Bernoulli applied Arbuthnot's significance test to a hypothesis about the planets (Freudenthal, 1970).

7. De Moivre–Laplace. Laplace cites De Moivre in his *Philosophical Essay on Probabilities*.

8. J. Bernoulli–Laplace. Laplace discusses Jacob Bernoulli's theorem in his *Philosophical Essay on Probabilities*.

9. D. Bernoulli–Laplace. Laplace cites Daniel Bernoulli in his *Philosophical Essay on Probabilities*.

10. Pascal–Laplace. Laplace discusses Pascal and Fermat in his *Philosophical Eusay on Probabilities*.

11. Pascal–Fermat. The well-known letters between Pascal and Fermat on gambling problems founded the field of probability.

12. Fermat–Laplace. Laplace discusses Pascal and Fermat in his *Philosophical Essay on Probabilities*.

13. De Moivre–De Morgan. De Morgan discusses the difficulty of De Moivre's proof (De Morgan, 1838).

14. Quetelet–De Morgan. Quetelet wrote De Morgan thanking him for sending him a table (Walker, 1929).

15. Laplace–Quetelet. Quetelet went to Paris and studied probability theory with Laplace.

16. Laplace–Gauss. Quetelet asked Napoleon to spare Gottingen because Gauss was there; Gauss discussed Laplace's books in class (Dunnington, 1955).

17. Gauss–Quetelet. Quetelet visited Gauss's observatory and the two discussed magnetism (ibid., 1955).

18. Gauss–Encke. Encke was a student of Gauss's (Walker, 1929).

19. Gauss–Bessel. Gauss and Bessel were lifelong friends (Dunnington, 1955).

20. Gauss–Kramp. Gauss developed a probability integral table based on Kramp's (Walker, 1929).

21. Bessel–Kramp. Bessel extended Kramp's probability integral table (ibid., 1929).

22. Encke–Kramp. Encke drew up probability integral tables based on an earlier table of Kramp's (Merriman, 1884).

23. De Morgan–Boole. De Morgan and Boole were firm friends (Broadbent, 1970).

24. Boole–Todhunter. Todhunter compiled a posthumous volume by Boole (ibid., 1970).

25. De Morgan–Todhunter. Todhunter's preface to his *History of Probability* expresses thanks for help to De Morgan.

26. Quetelet–Galton. Galton learned of the normal curve from Quetelet's *Letters ... on the Theory of Probability*.

27. Encke–Merriman. Merriman's *A Text-Book on the Method of Least Squares* presents normal curve tables on those of Encke.

28. Todhunter–Venn. Venn's (1888) preface to the first edition of *Logic of Chance* expresses thanks to Todhunter for reading proofs.

29. Venn–Edgeworth. Venn's preface to the third edition of *Logic of Chance* expresses thanks to Edgeworth for many discussions and for reading proofs.

30. Todhunter–Edgeworth. Edgeworth was influenced by Todhunter's *History of Probability* (Fitzpatrick, 1960).

31. Todhunter–Pearson. Pearson took the Smith's Prize exam from Todhunter and was later picked to finish his *History of the Theory of Elasticity*.

32. Edgeworth–Pearson. Edgeworth posed a question to Pearson that led to Pearson's family of frequency curves.

33. Galton-Pearson. Galton's *Natural Inheritance* was a major influence on Pearson's entire life's work.

34. Galton–Weldon. Weldon was inspired by Galton's *Natural Inheritance*; Galton was a referee on Weldon's first biometric paper.

35. Weldon–Pearson. Weldon went to Pearson for statistical advice and the two men became long-time partners in biometric research.

36. Pearson–Yule. Yule studied with Pearson and became his demonstrator.

37. Pearson–Fisher. Pearson published one of Fisher's first statistical papers. The two men later became involved in a number of emotional disputes over statistics.

38. Pearson–Gosset. Gosset went to Pearson for statistical help in the summer of 1905 and then spent most of a year at Pearson's Biometric Lab. The two had a strong lifelong relationship, and Gosset's pseudonym of "Student" was chosen to point out his indebtedness to Pearson.

39. Merriman–Gosset. Merriman's *A Text-Book on the Method of Least Squares* was one of the first sources to which Gosset turned for statistical help.

40. Gosset–Fisher. Fisher took Gosset's paper "On the Probable Error of a Mean" as the starting point for much of his own work. The two men were lifelong friends.

41. Fisher–Snedecor. Snedecor, along with Mahalanobis, improved the variance ratio statistic. Snedecor named it F in honor of Fisher.

Notes

Chapter 1

1. The Binomial Theroem states that for any real numbers a and b and for any positive integer n, $(a - b)$ to the nth power can be expanded into terms involving power of $a^v b^{n \times v}$ being $m!/v! (n \times v)!$. (See *Encyclopedia Britannica*, 15th ed., Micropaedia, Vol II, p. 25.)

Chapter 2

1. Writers in the eighteenth century did not take spelling seriously, and some authors would use Demoivre and Moivre in the same paragraph. De Moivre's own writings show that he never used Moivre alone, but that he did use several spellings, including de Moivre, Demoivre, and De Moivre (Walker, 1934). Sometimes De Moivre is alphabetized in reference works by Moivre and sometimes by De Moivre.

2. The complete text of De Moivre's translation of his paper into English can be found in Smith (1929, pp. 566-575) and David (1962, pp. 254-267).

Chapter 3

1. Lord Kelvin invented the absolute temperature scale and James Clerk Maxwell predicted the existence of radio waves on the basis of his analysis of mathematical equations. Todhunter wrote a famous history of probability and worked on the theories of elasticity.

2. Other wranlgers became lawyers. E. T. Bell writes, "It is somewhat astonishing to see how many of Engalnd's leading barristers and judges in the nineteenth century were high wranglers in the Cambridge tripos" (1937, p. 382)

Chapter 4

1. Because Karl Pearson's uon, Egon Sharpe Pearson, is himself a statistician of note, as well as the author or the major biographical work on his father, reference notes beginning with this chapter will refer to E. Pearson and K. Pearson.

2. Letter from E. S. Pearson to author, April 19, 1978.

Chapter 5

1. Letter from W. L. Bell, Information Officer University of Oxford, to author, December 4, 1978.

1. Letter from E. S. Pearson to author, June 28, 1977.

3. Information on the choice of the name "Student" came from a letter from Mrs. Eithne Mooney, Technical Information Officer, Arthur Guinness Sons & Co. (Dublin) Ltd., and from a note card on Gosset written by D. O. Williams, head brewer, and contained in the Guinness Museum.

4. Letter from E. S. Pearson, to author, June 28, 1977.

5. From a note card on Gosset written by D. O. williams, head brewer, and contained in the Guinness Museum.

6. Letter from E. S. Pearson to author, June 28, 1977.

Bibliography

Allen, R. G. D. 1971. Bowley, Sir Arthur Lyon. In *The dictionary of national biography, 1951-1960*, ed. E. T. Williams and Helen M. Palmer, pp. 133-135. London: Oxford University Press.

Arbuthnot, John, 1710. An argument for divine proficence, taken from the constant regularity observed in the births of both sexes. *Phil. Trans. Roy. Soc. London* 27:186-190.

Archibald, Raymond Clare. 1926. Abraham de Moivre. *Nature* 117:551.

————. 1949. *Outline of the history of mathematics*. 6th ed. Menasha, WI.: Mathematical Association of America.

Auden, W. H. 1966. *Collected shorter poems: 1927-1957*. New York: Random House.

Barbacki, S., and Fisher, R. A., 1936. A test of the supposed precision of systematic arrangements. *Ann. Eugenics* 7:189-193.

Barnard, G. A. (1958) 1970. Thomas Bayes — a biographical note. In *Studies in the History of Statistics and Probability*, ed. E. S. Pearson and M. G. Kendall, pp. 131-133. London: Charles Griffin and Co.

Bartlett, M. S. 1968. Fisher, R. A. In *International Encyclopedia of the Social Sciences*, ed. David L. Sills, vol. 5, pp. 485-491. New York: Macmillan and The Free Press.

Bateson, W. 1901. Heredity, differentiation and other conceptions of biology: A consideration of Professor Karl Pearson's paper "On the principle of homotyposis." *Proc. Roy. Soc. London* 69:193-205.

Bayes, Thomas. (1763) 1970. An essay towards solving a problem in the doctrine of chances. In *Studies in the History of Statistics and Probability*, ed. E. S. Pearson and M. G. Kendall, vol. 1, pp. 131-153. London: Charles Griffin and Co.

Beaver, Hugh. 1960. Presidential address: Statistics as a tool of management. *J. Roy. Statist. Soc.*, ser. A, 123:1-9.

Bell, E. T. (1937) 1965. *Men of mathematics*. New York: Simon and Schuster.

Beniger, James R.; and Robyn, Dorothy L. 1978. Quantitative graphics in statistics: A brief history. *The American Statistician* 32, no. 1:1-11.

Beveridge, W. I. B. (1950) 1957. *The art of scientific investigation*. New York: Vintage Books.

Bliss, C. I. 1967. *Statistics in biology: Statistical methods for research in the natural sciences*, vol. 1. New York: McGraw-Hill.

Block, N. J., and Dworkin, G. 1976. *The IQ controversy: Critical readings*. New York: Pantheon Books.

Boas, F. 1909. Determination of the coefficient of correlation. *Science* 29:823-824.

Boas, F. 1912. *Changes in bodily form of descendants of immigrants*. New York: Columbia University Press.

Bowley, A. L. 1935. Discussion on Professor Fisher's paper. *J. Roy. Statist. Soc.* 98:55-57.

Box, Joan Fisher. 1978. *R. A. Fisher: The life of a scientist.* New York: John Wiley & Sons, Inc.

Broadbent, T. A. A. 1970. Boole, George. In *Dictionary of scientific biography*, ed. Charles Coulston Gillispie, vol. 2, pp. 293-298. New York: Scribners.

Bronowski, J. (1956) 1965. *Science and human values.* New York: Harper & Row.

———— 1973. *The ascent of man.* Boston: Little, Brown, and Company.

Brown, B. W. 1972. Statistics, scientific method, and smoking. In *Statistics: A Guide to the Unknown*, ed. J. M. Tanur, F. Mosteller, W. H. Krushkal, et al., pp. 40-51. San Francisco: Holden-Day.

Bryan, William L. 1892. On the development of voluntary motor ability. *American Journal of Psychology* 5:125-204.

Burgess, Robert Wilbur. 1927. *Introduction to the mathematics of statistics.* Boston: Houghton Mifflin.

Burnside, W. 1923. On errors of observation. *Proc. Cambridge Phil. Soc* 21:482-487.

Campbell, Donald T., and Stanley, Julian C. 1966. *Experimental and quasi-experimental designs for research.* Chicago: Rand McNally.

Chang, Wei-Ching. 1976. Review of "The life and times of the central limit theorem." *Historia Mathematica* 3:353-354.

Chesterton, G. K. 1927. *Eugenics and other evils.* New York: Dodd, Mead and Company.

Clark, Ronald W. 1971. *Einstein: The life and times.* New York: Avon.

Clarke, Frances Marguerite. 1929. *Thomas Simpson and his times.* Baltimore: Waverly Press.

Clover, Vernon T., and Balsley, Howard L. 1974. *Business research methods.* Columbus, Ohio: Grid.

Cochran, William G. 1967. Footnote by William G. Cochran. *Science* 156:1460-1462.

————. 1976. Early development of techniques in comparative experimentation. In *On the History of Statistics and Probability*, ed. D. B. Owen, pp. 3-25. New York: Marcel Dekker.

Cornish, E. A. 1964. Fisher's activities in Australia, 1959-62. *Biometrics* 20:372-373.

Cowan, Ruth Schwartz. 1972. Francis Galton's statistical ideas: The influence of eugenics. *Isis* 63:509-528.

Craig, Allen T. 1960. Our silver anniversary. *Ann. Math. Stat.* 31:835-837.

Cunliffe, Stella V. 1976. Interaction: The address of the president. *J. Roy. Statist. Soc.*, ser. A. 139, part 1:1-19.

Darwin, Charles. (1876) 1900. *The effects of cross and self fertilisation in the vegetable kingdom.* 2nd ed. London: John Murray.

David, Florence N. 1962. *Games, gods and gambling: The origins and history of probability and statistical ideas from the earliest times to the Newtonian era.* New York: Hafner.

———. 1968. Galton, Francis. In *International Encyclopedia of the Social Sciences,* ed. David L. Sills, vol. 6, pp. 48-53. New York: Macmillan and The Free Press.

De Moivre, Abraham. (1738) 1959. On the law of normal probability. In *A Source Book in Mathematics.* ed. David E. Smith, vol. 2, pp. 566-575. New York: Dover.

De Morgan, Augustus. 1838. *An essay on probabilities and on their application to life contigencies and insurance offices.* London: Longman, Orme, Brown, Green & Longmans, and John Taylor.

Dempster, A. P. 1979. Life and work of Ronald Fisher. *Science* 203:537.

Deutsch, K. W.; Platt, J.; and Senghaas, D. 1971. Conditions favoring major advances in social science. *Science* 171:450-459.

Diamond, Solomon. 1969. Introduction. In L. A. J. Quetelet, *A Treatise on Man and the Development of his Faculties,* ed. Solomon Diamond, pp. v-xiii. Gainesville, Fla.: Scholars' Facsimiles and Reprints.

Dixon, Wilfrid, and Massey, Frank J., Jr. 1957. *Introduction to statistical analysis.* New York: McGraw-Hill.

Duggan, T. J., and Dean, D. W. 1968. Common misinterpretations of significance levels in sociological journals. *The American Sociologist* 3:45-46.

Dunnington, G. Waldo. 1955. *Carl Friedrich Gauss: Titan of science.* New York: Exposition Press.

Durkheim, Emile. (1897) 1966. *Suicide: A study in sociology.* New York: The Free Press.

E. M. E. 1938. Obituary: William Sealy Gosset, 187)-1937. *J. Roy. Statist. Soc.* 101:250-251.

Eden, T., and Fisher, R.A. 1927. Studies in crop variation. IV. The experimental determination of the value of top dressings with cereals. *J. Agr. Sci.* 17:548-562.

Edgeworth, F. Y. 1883. The method of least squares. *Phil. Mag.* 5th ser. 16:360-375.

———. 1885. Methods of statistics. *J. Roy. Statist. Soc.* Jubilee Volume: 181-217.

Edgington, E. S. 1964. A tabulation of inferential statistics used in psychology journals. *American Psychologist* 19:202-203.

———. 1974. A new tabulation of statistical procedures used in APA journals. *American Psychologist* 29:25-26.

Eisnhart, Churchill. 1968. Gauss, Carl Friedrich. In *International Encyclopedia of the Social Sciences,* ed. David L. Sills, vol. 6, pp. 78-81. Macmillan and The Free Press.

———. 1975. Review of "Statistical papers in honor of George W. Snedecor." *Historia Mathematica* 2:211-2181

———. 1979. On the transition from 'Student's' z to 'Student's' t. *The American Statistician* 33, no. 1:6-10.

Elderton, W. P. 1902. Tables for testing the goodness of fit of theory to observation. *Biometrika* 1:155-163.

Ellmann, Richard. 1959. *James Joyce*. New York: Oxford University Press.

———. ed. 1975. *Selected letters of James Joyce*. New York: University Press.

Eves, Howard. 1953. *An introduction to the history of mathematics*. New York: Rinehart and Co.

Fermat, Pierre de, and Pascal, Blaise. (1654) 1959. Fermat and Pascal on probability. In *A Source Book in Mathematics*, ed. David E. Smith, vol. 2, pp. 546-565. New York: Dover.

Finney, D. J. 1964a. Foreword: In memoriam Ronald Aylmer Fisher, 1890-1962. *Biometrics* 20:237.

———. 1964b. Sir Ronald Fisher's contributions to biometric statistics. *Biometrics* 20:322-329.

Fisher, R. A. 1912. On an absolute criterion for fitting frequency curves. *Messenger of Mathematics* 41:155-160.

———. 1914. Some hopes of a eugenist. *Eugenics Review* 5:309-315.

———. 1915. Frequency distribution of the values of the correlation coefficient in samples from a indefinitely large population. *Biometrika* 10:507-521.

———. 1917. Positive eugenics. *Eugenics Review* 9:206-212.

———. 1918. The correlation between relatives on the supposition of Mendelian inheritance. *Trans. Roy. Soc. Edinburgh* 52:399-433.

———. 1921. Studies in crop variation. I. An examination of the yield of dressed grain from Brodbalk. *J. Agr. Sci.* 11:107-135.

———. 1922a. The evolution of the conscience in civilized communities: In special relation to sexual vices. *Eugenics Review* 14:180-193.

———. 1922b. On the interpretation of x^2 from contingency tables, and the calculation of P. *J. Roy. Statist. Soc.* 85:87-94.

———. 1923. Note on Dr. Burnside's recent paper on errors of observation. *Proc. Cambridge Phil. Soc.* 21:655-658.

———. 1924a. The conditions under which x^2 measures the discrepancy between observation and hypothesis. *J. Roy. Statist. Soc.* 87:442-450.

———. (1924b) 1950. On a distribution yielding the error functions of several well known statistics. In R. A. Fisher, ed., *Contributions to Mathematical Statistics*, pp. 12.804a-12.813. New York: John Wiley & Sons, Inc.

———. 1924c. The influence of rainfall on the yield of wheat at Rothmasted. *Phil. Trans. Roy. Soc. London*, ser. B, 213:89-142.

———. 1925a. Applications of "Student's" distribution. *Metron* 5, no. 3:90-104.

———. (1925b) 1928. *Statistical methods for research workers*. 2nd ed.

London: Oliver and Boyd.

————. (1925c) 1958. *Statistical methods for research workers*. 13th ed. New York: Hafner.

————. (1926) 1950. The arrangement of field experiments. In R. A. Fisher, ed., *Contributions to Mathematical Statistics*, pp. 17.50a-17.513. New York: John Wiley & Sons, Inc.

————. 1929. Balance of births and deaths. *Eugenics Review* 12:236.

————. (1930) 1950. Moments and product moments of sampling distributions. In R. A. Fisher, ed., *Contributions to Mathematical Statistics*, pp. 20.198a-20.238. New York: John Wiley & Sons, Inc.

————. 1933. Number of Mendelian factors in quantitative inheritance. *Nature* 131:400-401.

————. (1953a) 1966. *The design of experiments*. 8th ed. New York: Hafner.

————. 1953b. The logic of inductive inference. *J. Roy. Statist. Soc.* 98:39-54.

————. 1936. The use of multiple measurements in taxonomic problems. *Ann. Eugenics* 7:179-188.

————. (1937) 1950. Professor Karl Pearson and the method of moments. In R. A. Fisher, ed., *Contributions to Mathematical Statistics*, pp. 29.302a-29.318. New York: John Wiley & Sons, Inc.

————. 1938. On the statistical treatment of the relation between sea-level characteristics and high-altitude acclimatization. *Proc. Roy. Soc. London, ser B*, 126:25-29.

————. 1939. "Student." *Ann. Eugenics* 9:1-9.

————. 1940. The precision of discriminant functions. *Ann. Eugenics* 10:422-429.

————. (1948) 1964. Biometry. *Biometrics* 20:261-264.

————. 1950. *Contributions to mathematical statistics*. New York: John Wiley & Sons, Inc.

————. (1956) 1959. *Statistical methods and scientific inference*. 2nd ed. New York: Hafner.

————. 1958a. Lung cancer and cigarettes? *Nature* 181:108.

————. 1958b. Cancer and smoking. *Nature* 182:596.

Fisher, R.A., and Bartlett, S. 1931. Pasteurized and raw milk. *Nature* 127:591-592.

Fisher, R. A., and MacKenzie, W. A. 1923. Studies in crop variation. II. The manurial response of different potato varieties. *J. Agr. Sci.* 13:311-320.

Fitzpatrick, Paul J. (1960) 1977. Leading British statisticians of the nineteenth century. In *Studies in the History of Statistics and Probability*, eds., Maurice Kendall and R. L. Plackett, vol. 2, pp. 180-212. London: Charles Griffin and Co.

Forrest, D. W. 1974. *Francis Galton: The life and work of a Victorian genius.* New York: Taplinger Pubushing Co.

Fréchet, Maruice. 1968. Laplace, Pierre Simon de. In *International Encyclopedia of the Social Sciences,* ed. David L. Sills, vol. 9, pp. 23-27. New York: Macmillan and The Free Press.

Freudenthal, Hans. 1970. Arbuthnot, John. In *Dictionary of Scientific Biography,* ed. Charles Coulston Gillisie, vol. 1, pp. 208-209. New York: Scribners.

Freund, John E. 1960. *Modern elementary statistics.* 2nd ed. Englewood Cliffs, N.J.: Prentice-Hall.

Galton, Francis. 1865a. On spectacles for divers and on the vision of amphibious animals. *Brit. Assoc. Rep.* 35:10-11.

———. 1865b. On stereoscopic maps, taken from models of mountainous countries. *Journal of the Geographical Society* 35:99-104.

———. 1865c. Hereditary talent and character. *Macmillan's Magazine* 12:157-166, 318-327.

———. (1869) 1870. *Hereditary genius: Its laws and consequences.* New York: D Appleton & Co.

———. 1870. Barometric predictions of weather. *Nature* 2:501-403.

———. 1872. Statistical inquiries into the efficacy of prayer. *Fortnightly Review* 12:125-135.

———. 1874. *English men of science: Their nature and nurture.* London: Macmillan.

———. 1875. The history of twins, as a criterion of the relative powers of nature and nurture. *Fraser's magazine* 92:566-576.

———. (1883) 1907. *Inquiries into human faculty and its development.* London: J. M. Dent & Sons.

———. 1885a. The measure of fidget. *Nature* 32:174-175.

———. 1885b. Regression towards mediocrity in hereditary stature. *Journal of the Anthropological Institute* 15:246-263.

———. 1885b. Regression towards mediocrity in hereditary stature. *Journal of the Anthropological Institute* 15:246-263.

———. 1886a. Family likeness in stature, with an appendix by J. D. Hamilton Dickson. *Proc. Roy. Soc. London* 40:42-73.

———. 1886b. President's address. *Journal of the Anthropological Institute* 15:489-499.

———. 1888. Co-relations and their measurement, chiefly from anthropometric data. *Proc. Roy. Soc. London* 45:135-145.

———. 1889. *Natural inheritance.* London: Macmillan.

———. 1892. *Finger prints.* London: Macmillan.

———. 1896. Intelligible signals between neighboring stars. *Fortnightly Review* 66:657-664.

———. 1899. A geometric determination of the median value of a system of normal variants, from two of its centiles. *Nature* 61:102-104.

———. 1901. Biometry. *Biometrika* 1:7-10.

————. 1905. Number of strokes of the brush in a picture. Nature 72:198.

————. 1906. Cutting a round cake on scientific principles. Nature 75:173.

————. 1908. Memories of my life, 2nd ed. London: Methuen & Co.

Gosset, William Sealy (Student). 1907. On the error of counting with a heamacytometer. Biometrika 5:351-360.

————. 1908a. The probable error of a mean. Biometrika 6:1125.

————. 1908b. Probable error of a correlation coefficient. Biometrika 6:302-310.

————. 1909. The distribution of the means of samples which are not drawn at random. Biometrika 7:210-214.

————. (1911) 1958. Appendix to Mercer and Hall's paper on "The experimental error of field trials." In "Student's" Collected Papers, ed. E. S. Pearson and John Wishart, pp. 49-52. Cambridge: Cambridge University Press.

————.1913. The correction to be made to the correlation ratio for grouping. Biometrika 9:316-320.

————. 1914. The elimination of spurious correlation due to position in time or space. Biometrika 10:179-180.

————. 1917. Tables for estimating the probability that the mean of a unique sample of observations lies between $-\infty$ and any given distance of the mean of the population from which the sample is drawn. Biometrika 11:414-417.

————. 1919. An explanation of deviations from Poisson's law in practice. Biometrika 12:211-215.

————. 1921. An experimental determination of the probable error of Dr. Spearman's correlation coefficients. Biometrika 13:263-282.

————. 1923. On testing varieties of cereals. Biometrika 15:271-293.

————. 1924. Note by "Student" with regard to his paper "On testing varieties of cereals." Biometrika 16:411.

————. 1925. New tables for testing the significance of observations. Metron 5, no. 3:105-108.

————. (1926a) 1958. Mathematics and agronomy. In "Student's " Collected Papers, ed. E. S. Pearson and John Wishart, pp. 121-134. Cambridge: Cambridge University Press.

————. 1926b. Review of Statistical Methods for Research Workers, by R. A. Fisher. Eugenics Review 18:148-150.

————. 1927. Errors of routine analysis. Biometrika 19:151-164.

————. 1929a. Statistics in biological research. Nature 124:93.

————. 1929b. Review of The Balance of Birth and Deaths: Vol. I. Western and Northern Europe, by Robert R. Kuczynski. Eugenics Review 12:130-131.

————. (1930) 1958. Agricultural field expermients. In "Student's" Collected Papers, ed. E. S. Pearson and John Wishart, pp. 216-217. Cambridge: Cambridge University Press.

———. 1931a. The Lanarkshire milk experiment. *Biometrika* 23:398-406.

———. 1931b. On the "z" test. *Biometrika* 23:407-408.

———. (1931c) 1958. Agricultural field experiments. In "*Student's*" *Collected Papers*, ed. E. S. Pearson and John Wishart, pp. 217-218. Cambridge: Cambridge University Press.

———. (1931d) 1958. Yield trials. In "*Student's*" *Collected Papers*, ed. E. S. Pearson and John Wishart, pp. 150-168. Cambridge: Cambridge University Press.

———. 1933. Evolution by selection. The implications of Winter's selection experiment. *Eugenics Review* 24:293-296.

———. (1934a) 1958. Contribution to a discussion at a meeting of the industrial and agricultural research section of the Royal Statistical Society. In "*Student's*" *Collected Papers*, ed. E. S. Pearson and John Wishart, pp. 220-221. Cambridge: Cambridge University Press.

———. 1934b. A calculation of the minimum number of genes in Winter's selection experiment. *Ann. Eugenics* 6:77-82.

———. (1936a) 1958. Co-operation in large-scale experments. A discussion by W. S. Gosset. In "*Student's*" *Collected Papers*, ed. E. S. Pearson and John Wishart, pp. 192-198. Cambridge: Cambridge University Press.

———. (1936b) 1958. The half-drill strip system agricultural experiments. In "*Student's*" *Collected Papers*, ed. E. S. Pearson and John Wishart, pp. 218-219. Cambridge: Cambridge University Press.

———. (1936c) 1958. Contribution to a discussion at a meeting of the industrial and agricultural research section of the Royal Statistical Society. In "*Student's*" *Collected Papers*, ed. E. S. Pearson and John Wishart, pp. 221-222. Cambridge: Cambridge University Press.

———. (1937a) 1958. Contribution to a discussion at a meeting of the industrial and agricultural research section of the Royal Statistical Society. In "*Student's*" *Collected Papers*, ed. E. S. Pearson and John Wishart, p. 222. Cambridge: Cambridge University Press.

———. (1937b) 1958. Contribution to a discussion at a meeting of the industrial and agricultural research section of the Royal Statistical Society. In "*Student's*" *Collected Papers*, ed., E. S. Pearson and John Wishart, pp. 223-224. Cambridge: Cambridge University Press.

———. 1937c. Comparison between balanced and random arrangements of field plots. *Biometrika* 29:363-379.

Gosset, W. S. 1970. *Letters from W. S. Gosset to R. A. Fisher, 1915-1936.* With summaries by R. A. Fisher and a foreword by L. McMullen. Issued for private circulation. Dublin: Arthur Guinness Sons & Co. (Dublin) Ltd.

Gossett, Thomas F. 1963. *Race: The history of an idea in America.* Dallas: Southern Methodist Univierstiy Press.

Graham, Kenneth R. 1977. *Psychological research: Controlled interpersonal interaction.* Monterey, Calif.: Brooks/Cole.

Graunt, John. (1662) 1975. *Natural and political observations mentioned in a following index and made upon the bills of mortality.* New York: Arno Press.

Greenwood, M. 1949. Pearson, Karl. In *The Dictionary of National Biography, 1931-40*, ed. L. G. Wickham Legg, pp. 681-684. London: Oxford University Press.

Guilford, J. P. 1936. *Psychometric methods.* New York: McGraw-Hill.

Guilford, J. P., and Fruchter, Benjamin. 1973. *Fundamental statistics in*

Heilbroner, Robert L. (1953) 1967. *The worldly philosophers: The lives, times, and ideas of the great economic thinkers.* 3rd ed. New York: Simon and Schuster.

Heyde, C. C., and Seneta, E. 1977. *I. J. Bienaymé: Statistical theory anticipated.* New York: Springer-Verlag.

Hilts, Victor L. 1973. Statistics and social science. In *Foundations of Scientific Method: The Nineteenth Century*, ed. Ronald F. Giere and Richard S. Westfall, pp. 206-233. Bloomington, Ind.: Indiana University Press.

Hogan, Edward R. 1977. Robert Adrain: American mathematician. *Historia Mathematica* 4:157-172.

Hogben, Lancelot. 1957. *Statistical theory: The relationship of probability, credibility and error.* London: George Allen & Unwin Ltd.

———. 1960. *Mathematics in the making.* London: Macdonald. Hopkins, Kenneth D., and Glass, Gene V. 1978. *Basic statistics for the behavioral sciences.* Englewood Cliffs, N. J.: Prentice-Hall.

psychology and education. New York: McGraw-Hill.

H. H. 1938. Obituary: William Sealy Goxset, 1876-1937. *J. Roy. Statist. Soc.* 101:248-249.

Hacking, Ian. 1965. *Logic of statistical inference.* Cambridge: Cambridge University Press.

———. 1970. Bayes, Thomas. In *Dictionary of Scientific Biography*, ed. Charles Coulston Gillispie, vol. 1, pp. 531-532. New York: Scribners.

Hadamard, Jacques. (1945) 1954. *An essay on the psychology of invention in the mathematical field.* New York: Dover.

Haldane, J. B. S. (1957) 1970. Karl Pearson, 1857 (1957). In *Studies in the History of Statistics and Probability*, ed. E. S. Pearson and M. G. Kendall, Vol. 1, pp. 427-437. London: Charles Griffin and Co.

Hall, Tord. 1970. *Carl Griedrich Gauss.* Cambridge, Mass.: The MIT Press.

Halley, Edmund. 1693. An estimate of the degrees of mortality of mankind drawn from curious tables of the births and funerals at the city of Breslaw, with an attempt to ascertain the price of annuities upon lives. *Phil. Trans. Roy. Soc. London* 17: 596-610.

Hammond, Kenneth R.; Householder, James E.; and Castellan, N. John, Jr.

1970. *Introduction to the statistical method: Foundations and use in the behavioral sciences.* 2nd ed. New York: Knopf.

Hankins, Frank H. 1908. Adolphe Quetelet as statistician. *Studies in History, Economics and Public Law* 31, no. 4: 443-576.

Hardy, G. H. (1940) 1967. *A mathematician's apology.* Cambridge: Cambridge University Press.

Harshbarger, Boyd. 1976. History of the early developments of modern statistics in America (1920-1944). In *On the History of Statistics and Probability*, ed. D. B. Owen, pp. 133-145. New York: Marcel Dekker.

Hays, William L. 1963. *Statistics for psychologists.* New York: Holt, Rinehart, and Winston.

————. (1963a) 1970. Ronald Aylmer Fisher, 1890-1962. In *Studies in the History of Statistics and Probability*, ed. E. S. Pearson and M. G. Kendall, vol. 1, pp. 439-453. London: Charles Griffin and Co.

————. (1963b) 1970. Isaac Todhunter's history of the mathematical theory of probability. In *Studies in the History of Statistics and Probability*, ed. E. S. Pearson and M. G. Kendall, vol. 1, pp. 253-254. London: Charles Griffin and Co.

————. 1968a. The history of statistical method. In *International Encyclopedia of the Social Sciences*, ed. David L. Sills, vol. 15, pp. 224-232. New York: Macmillan and The Free Press.

————. (1968b) 1970. Francis Ysidro Edgeworth, 1845-1926. In *Studies in*

Hotelling, H. 1931. Recent improvements in statistical inference. *J. Am. Statist. Assoc.* 26:79-87.

————. 1951. The impact of R. A. Fisher on statistics. *J. Am. Statist. Assoc.* 46:35-46.

Irwin, J. O. 1968. Gosset, William Sealy. In *International Encyclopedia of the Social Sciences*, ed. David L. Sills, vol. 6, pp. 211-214. New York: Macmillan and The Free Press.

James, Glenn, and James, R. C., eds. 1968. *Mathematics dictionary.* 3rd ed. Princeton: D. Van Nostrand.

Janik, Allan, and Toulmin, Stephen. 1973. *Wittgenstein's Vienna.* New York: Simon and Schuster.

Jensen, A. 1969. How much can we boost I.Q. and scholastic achievement? *Harvard Educational Review* 39, no. 1:1-123.

Johnson, Marcia K., and Liebert, Robert M. 1977. *Statistics: Tool of the Behavioral Sciences.* Englewood Cliffs, N. J.: Prentice-Hall.

Kac, Mark. 1964. Probability. *Scientific American* 211, no. 3: 92-108.

Karush, William. 1962. *The crescent dictionary of mathematics.* New York: Macmillan.

Kempthorne, O. 1966. Some aspects of experimental inference. *J. Am. Statist. Assoc.* 61:11-334.

————. 1976. The analysis of variance and factorial design. In *On the History of Statistics and Probability*, ed. D. B. Owen, pp. 29-54. New York:

Marcel Dekker.

Kendall, Maurice G. 1948. *The advanced theory of statistics*. 4th ed. London: Charles Griffin and Co.

————. (1952) 1970. George Udny Yule, 1871-1951. In *Studies in the History of Statistics and Probability*, ed. E. S. Pearson and M. G. Kendall, vol. 1, pp. 419-425. London: Charles Griffin and Co.

————. (1956) 1970. The beginnings of a probability calculus. In *Studies in the History of Statistics and Probability*, ed. E. S. Pearson and M. G. Kendall, vol. 1, pp. 19-34. London: Charles Griffin and Co.

————. (1961) 1970. Daniel Bernoulli on maximum likelihood. In *Studies in the History of Statistics and Probability*, ed. E. S. Pearson and M. G. Kendall, vol. 1, pp. 155-156. London: Charles Griffin and Co.

the History of Statistics and Probability, ed. E. S. Pearson and M. G. Kendall, vol. 1, pp. 257-263. London: Charles Griffin and Co.

————. 1972. The history and future of statistics. In *Statistical Papers in Honor of George W. Snedecor*, ed. T. A. Bancroft assisted by Susan Alice Brown, pp. 193-210. Ames, Iowa: Iowa State University Press.

————. 1976. Statisticians — Production and consumption. *The American Statistician* 30, no. 2:49-53.

Kendall, Maurice G., and Buckland, William R. 1957. *A dictionary of statistical terms*. London: Charles Griffin and Co.

Kendall, Maurice, and Plackett, R.L., eds. 1977. *Studies in the history of statistics and probability*, vol. 2. London: Charles Griffin and Co.

Kerlinger, Fred N., and Pedhazur, Elazar J. 1973. *Multiple regression in behavioral research*. New York: Holt, Rinehart, and Winston.

Kevles, Daniel J. (1978) 1979. *The physicists: The history of a scientific community in modern America*. New York: Vintage Books.

Keys, Ancel; Matthews, Bryan H. C.; Forbes, W. H.; and MacFarland, Ross A. 1938. Individual variations in ability to acclimatize to high altitude. *Proc. Roy. Soc. London*, ser. B, 126:1-24.

Kimble, Gregory A. 1978. *How to use (and misuse) statistics*. Englewood Cliffs, N.J.: Prentice-Hall.

Kirk, Roger E. 1978. *Introductory statistics*. Monterey, Calif.: Brooks/Cole.

Kline, Morris. (1953) 1977. *Mathematics in western culture*. Harmondsworth, Middlesex: Penguin Books.

Koren, John. 1918. *The history of statistics, their development and progress in many countries; in memoirs to commemorate the seventy fifth anniversary of the American Statistical Association*. New York: Macmillan.

Koshal, R. S. 1933. Application of the method of maximum likelihood to the improvement of curves fitted by the method of moments. *J. Roy. Statist. Soc.* 96:303-313.

Kruskal, William H. (1965) 1967. Statistics, Moliere, and Henry Adams. *American Scientist* 55:416-428.

————. 1968. Statistics: The field. In *International Encyclopedia of the Social Sciences*, ed. David L. Sills, vol. 15, pp. 206-224. New York: Macmillan and The Free Press.

Kuhn, Thomas S. 1962. *The structure of scientific revolutions*. Chicago: The University of Chicago Press.

————. 1977. *The essential tension: Selected studies in scientific tradition and change*. Chicago: The University of Chicago Press.

Lachenbruch, P. A. 1975. *Discriminant analysis*. New York: Hafner.

Landau, David, and Lazarsfeld, Paul F. 1968. Quetelet, Adolphe. In *International Encyclopedia of the Social Sciences*, ed. David L. Sills, vol. 13, pp. 247-257. New York: Macmillan and The Free Press.

Laplace, Pierre Simon. (1814) 1951. *A philosophical essay on probabilities*. New York: Dover.

Lawes, J. B., and Gilbert, J. H. 1880. Agricultural, botanical, and chemical results of experiments on the mixed herbiage of permanent meadow, conducted for more than twenty years on the same land — Part I. *Phil. Trans. Roy. Soc. London* 171, part 1: 289-416.

Lee, Eui Bun, and Olkes, Cheryl. 1976. How statistical techniques vary in four journals. *Journalism Educator* 31, no. 3:54-56.

Lindquist, E. F. 1940. *Statistical analysis in educational research*. Boston: Houghton Mifflin.

Lundberg, George A. 1940. Statistics in modern social thought. In *Contemporary Social Theory*, ed. Harvey E. Barnes, Howard Becker and Frances B. Becker, pp. 110-140. New York: D. Appleton-Century Co.

Lush, Jay L. 1972. Early statistics at Iowa State University. In *Statistical Papers in Honor of George W. Snedecor*, ed. T. A. Bancroft assisted by Susan Alice Brown, pp. 211-226. Ames, Iowa: Iowa University Press.

McCall, W. A. 1923. *How to experiment in education*. New York: Macmillan.

McMullen, Launce. (1939) 1970. William Sealy Gosset, 1876-1937. (1) "Student" as a man. In *Studies in the History of Statistics and Probability*, ed. E. S. Pearson and M. G. Kendall, vol. 1, pp. 355-360. London: Charles Griffin and Co.

————. 1958. Foreword. In *"Student's" Collected Papers*, ed. E. S. Pearson and John Wishart, 3rd ed., pp. xi-xvi. Cambridge: Cambridge University Press.

McNemar, Quinn. 1949. *Psychological statistics*. New York: John Wiley & Sons, Inc.

————. 1962. *Psychological statistics*. 3rd ed. New York: John Wiley & Sons, Inc.

Mach, Ernst. (1883) 1942. *The science of mechanics*. London: The Open Court Publishing Co.

————. 1902. *Die Analyse der Empfindungen und das Verhaltniss des Physischen zum Psychischen*. Gena: G. Fischer.

Mack, Sidney. 1960. Elementary statistics. New York: Henry Holt.

MacKenzie, D. 1976. Eugenics in Britain. Social Studies of Science 6:499-532.

———. 1978. Statistical theory and social interests: A case-study. Social Studies of Science 8, no. 1:35-83.

Mahalanobis, P. C. (1938) 1950. Professor Ronald Aylmer Fisher. In Contributions to Mathematical Statistics, ed. R. A. Fisher, pp. 265-272. New York: John Wiley & Sons, Inc.

———. 1964. Some personal memories of R. A. Fisher. Biometrics 20:368-371.

Maistrov, L. E. 1974. Probability theory: A historical sketch, edited and translated by Samuel Kotz. New York: Academic Press.

Mantel, Nathan. 1976. A personal perspective on statistical techniques for quasi-experiments. In On the History of Statistics and Probability, ed. D. B. Owen, pp. 103-129. New York: Marcel Dekker.

Marascuilo, Leonard A. and McSweeney, Maryellen. 1977. Nonparametric and distribution-free methods for the social sciences. Monterey, Calif.: Brooks/Cole.

Mather, K. 1964. R. A. Fisher's work in genetics. Biometrics 20:330-342.

May, Kenneth O. 1972. Gauss, Carl Friedrich. In Dictionary of Scientific Biography, ed. Charles Coulston Gillispie, vol. 5, pp. 298-315. New York: Scribners.

Medawar, Peter B., and Medawar, Jean S. 1977. Revising the facts of life. Harper's 254, no. 1521:41-60.

Meier, P. 1972. The biggest public health experiment ever: The 1954 field trial of the Salk poliomyelitis vaccine. In Statistics: A Guide to the Unknown, ed. J. M. Tanur, F. Mosteller, W. H. Kruskal, et al., pp. 2-13. San Francisco: Holden-Day.

Meitzen, August. 1891. History, theory and technique of statistics, translated by Roland P. Falkner. Philadelphia: Academy of Political and Social Science.

Merriman, Mansfield. (1884) 1911. A text-book on the method of least squares. 8th ed. New York: John Wiley & Sons, Inc.

Michell, John. 1767. An inquiry into the probable parallax, and magnitude of the fixed stars, from the quantity of light which they afford us, and the particular circumstances of their situation. Phil. Trans. Roy. Soc. London 57:234-264.

Miller, George A., and Buckhout, Robert. 1973. Psychology: The science of mental life. 2nd ed. New York: Harper & Row.

Mills, Frederick C. 1955. Statistical methods. 3rd ed. New York: Henry Holt.

Mood, Alexander McFarlane. 1950. Introduction to the theory of statistics. New York: McGraw-Hill.

Morgan, Bryan. 1972. Men and discoveries in mathematics. London: John

Murray.

Moroney, M. J. 1951. *Facts from figures*. Baltimore: Penguin Books.

Neyman, J. 1938. Mr. W. S. Gosset. *J. Am. Statist. Assoc.* 33:226-228.

———. 1967. R. A. Fisher (1890-1962): An appreciation. *Science* 156:1456-1460.

———. 1976. The emergence of mathematical statistics: A historical sketch with particular reference to the United States. In *On the History of Statistics and Probability*, ed. D. B. Owen, pp. 149-193. New York: Marcel Dekker.

Neyman, J., and Pearson, E. S. 1936. *Statistical research memoirs*, vol. 1. Cambridge: Cambridge University Press.

———. 1937. Note on some points in "Student's" paper on "Comparison between balanced and random arrangements of field plots." *Biometrika* 29:380-388.

Norton, Bernard J. 1978. Karl Pearson and statistics: The social origins of scientific innovation. *Social Studies of Science* 8, no. 1:3-34.

Ore, Oystein. 1960. Pascal and the invention of probability theory. *Amer. Math. Monthly* 67:409-419.

———. 1968. Bernoulli family. In *International Encyclopedia of the Social Sciences*, ed. David L. Sills, vol. 2, pp. 65-68. New York: Macmillan and the Free Press.

Osborn, Frederick Henry. 1978. Eugenics. The *Encyclopaedia Britannica, Macropaedia*, vol. 6, pp. 1023-1026.

Ostle, Bernard. 1954. *Statistics in research: Basic concepts and techniques for research workers*. Ames, Iowa: Iowa State University Press.

Owen, Donald B. 1968. Special continuous distributions. In *International Encyclopedia of the Social Sciences*, ed. David L. Sills, vol. 4, pp. 223-230. New York: Macmillan and The Free Press.

———, ed. 1976. *On the history of statistics and probability*. New York: Marcel Dekker.

Pearson, Egon Sharpe. 1937. Mr. W. S. Gosset: "Student." *Nature* 140:838.

———. 1938. *Karl Pearson: An appreciation of some aspects of his life and work*. Cambridge: Cambridge University Press.

———. (1939) 1970. William Sealy Gosset, 1876-1937. (2) "Student" as a statistician. In *Studies in the History of Statistics and Probability*, ed. E. S. Pearson and M. G. Kendall, vol. 1, pp. 360-403. London: Charles Griffin and Co.

———, ed. (1948) 1956. *Karl Pearson's early statistical papers*. Cambridge: Cambridge University Press.

———. (1965) 1970. Some incidents in the early history of biometry and statistics. In *Studies in the History of Statistics and Probability*, ed. E. S. Pearson and M. G. Kendall, vol. 1, pp. 323-338. London: Charles Griffin and Co.

————. (1966) 1970. The Neyman-Pearson story: 1926-34. Historical sidelights on an episode in Anglo-Polish collaboration. In *Studies in the History of Statistics and Probability*, ed. E. S. Pearson and M. G. Kendall, vol. 1, pp. 455-477. London: Charles Griffin and Co.

————. (1967) 1970. Some reflections on continuity in the development of mathematical statistics, 1885-1920. In *Studies in the History of Statistics and Probability*, ed. E. S. Pearson and M. G. Kendall, vol. 1, pp. 339-353. London: Charles Griffin and Co.

————. (1968) 1970. Some early correspondence between W. S. Gosset, R. A. Fisher and Karl Pearson, with notes and comments. In *Studies in the History of Statistics and Probability*, ed. E. S. Pearson and M. G. Kendall, vol. 1, pp. 405-417. London: Charles Griffin and Co.

Pearson, E. S., and Kendall, M. G., eds. 1970. *Studies in the History of Statistics and Probability*, vol. 1. London: Charles Griffin and Co.

Pearson, E. S., and Wishart, John, eds. (1907-1938) 1958. "*Student's*" collected papers. 3rd ed. Cambridge: Cambridge University Press.

Pearson, Karl. (1892) 1911. *The grammar of science*. 3rd ed. New York: Macmillan.

————. 1893. Contributions to the mathematical theory of evolution. *Proc. Roy. Soc. London* 54:329-333.

————. 1894. Contributions to the mathematical theory of evolution. *Phil. Trans. Roy. Soc. London*, ser. A, 185:71-110.

————. 1895a. Contributions to the mathematical theory of evolution — II. Skew variations in homogeneous material. *Phil. Trans. Roy. Soc. London*, ser. A, 186:343-414.

————. 1895b. Note on regression and inheritance in the case of two parents. *Proc. Roy. Soc. London* 58:240-242.

————. 1896. Mathematical contributions to the theory of evolution — III. Regression, heredity and panmixia. *Phil. Trans. Roy. Soc. London*, ser. A, 187:253-318.

————. 1897. Mathematical contributions to the theory of evolution — On a form of spurious correlation which may arise when indices are used in the measurement of organs. *Proc. Roy. Soc. London* 60:489-498.

————. (1898) 1956. Mathematical contributions to the theory of evolution — V. On the reconstruction of the stature of prehistoric races. In *Karl Pearson's Early Statistical Papers*, ed. E. S. Pearson, pp. 263-338. Cambridge: Cambridge University Press.

————. 1900. On the criterion that a given system of deviations from the probable in the case of a correlated system of variables is such that it can be reasonably supposed to have arisen from random sampling. *Phil. Mag.* 5th ser. 50:157-175.

————. 1901. Mathematical contributions to the theory of evolutions — VII. On the correlation of characters not quantitatively measurable. *Phil. Trans. Roy. Soc. London* A 195:1-47.

———. 1903. On the inheritance of the mental and moral characters in man, and its comparison with the inheritance of the physical characters. *Journal of the Anthropological Institute* 33:179-237.

———. (1904) 1956. Mathematical contributions to the theory of evolution — XIII. On the theory of contingency and its relation to association and normal correlation. In *Karl Pearson's Early Statistical Papers*, ed. E. S. Pearson, pp. 443-475. Cambridge: Cambridge University Press.

———. (1906) 1970. Walter Frank Raphael Weldon, 1860-1906. In *Studies in the History of Statistics and Probability*, ed. E. S. Pearson and M. G. Kendall, vol. 1, pp. 265-321. London: Charles Griffin and Co.

———. 1909. Letter to the editor: Determination of the coefficient of correlation. *Science* 30:23-25.

———. 1914. *The life, letters and labours of Francis Galton*, vol. 1. Cambridge: Cambridge University Press.

———. (1916) 1956. Mathematical contributions to the theory of evolution — XIX. Second supplement to a memoir on skew variation. In *Karl Pearson's Early Statistical Papers*, ed. E. S. Pearson, pp. 529-557. Cambridge: Cambridge University Press.

———. (1920) 1970. Notes on the history of correlation. In *Studies in the History of Statistics and Probability*, ed. E. S. Pearson and M. G. Kendall, vol. 1, pp. 185-205. London: Charles Griffin and Co.

———. 1924a. Historical note on the origin of the normal curve of errors. *Biometrika* 16:402-404.

———. 1924b. *The life, letters and labours of Francis Galton*, vol. 2. Cambridge: Cambridge University Press.

———. 1925. James Bernoulli's theorem. *Biometrika* 17:201-210.

———. 1926. Abraham de Moivre. *Nature* 117:551-552.

———. 1929. Statistics in biological research. *Nature* 124:183.

———. 1930a. *The life, letters and labours of Francis Galton*, vol. 3A. Cambridge: Cambridge University Press.

———. 1930b. *The life, letters and labours of Francis Galton*, vol. 3B. Cambridge: Cambridge University Press.

———. 1931a. On the nature of the relationship between two of "Student's" variates (z^1 and z^2) when samples are taken from a bivariate normal population. *Biometrika* 22:405-422.

———. 1931b. Further remarks on the "z" test. *Biometrika* 23:408-415.

———. 1936a. Old Tripos days at Cambridge, as seen from another viewpoint. *Mathematical Gazette* 20:27-36.

———. 1936b. Method of moments and method of maximum likelihood. *Biometrika* 28:34-59.

———. 1978. *The history of statistics in the 17th and 18th centuries against the changing background of intellectual, scientific and religious thought. Lectures by Karl Pearson given at University College London during the academic sessions 1921-1933*, ed. E. S. Pearson. New

York: Macmillan.

Pearson, K., and Morant, G. M. 1934. The Wilkinson head of Oliver Cromwell and its relationship to busts, masks and painted portraits. *Biometrika* 26:269-378.

Peters, Charles C., and Van Voorhis, Walter R. 1940. *Statistical procedures and their mathematical bases.* New York: McGraw-Hill.

Petty, Sir William. (1690) 1883. Political arithmetic, or a discourse concerning the extent and value of lands, people, buildings; husbandry, manufacture, commerce, fishery, artisans, seamen, soldiers; public revenues, interest, taxes, superlucration, registries, banks; valuation of men, increasing of seamen; of militias, harbours, situation, shipping, power at sea, etc: as the same relates to every country in general, but more particularly to the territories of his majesty of Great Britain, and his neighbors of Holland, Zealand, and France. In *An English Garner: Ingatherings from Our History and Literature,* ed. Edward Arber, vol. 6, pp. 323-388. Birmingham: E. Arber.

Plackett, R. L. 1972. Studies in the history of probability and statistics. XXIX. The discovery of the method of least squares. *Biometrika* 59:239-251.

Polya, G. 1973. *How to solve it: A new aspect of mathematical method.* 2nd ed. Princeton, N.J.: Princeton University Press.

Porter, D. Thomas. 1977. Toward an idolatry of "p." *Journal of Communication* 27:238-39.

Quetelet, Lambert Adolphe Jacques. (1842) 1969. *A treatise on man and the development of his faculties.* Gainesville, Fla.: Scholars' Facsimiles and Reprints.

————. 1849. *Letters addressed to H.R.H. the Grand Duke of Saxe Coburg and Gotha, on the theory of probabilities, as applied to the moral and political sciences,* translated by Olinthus Gregory Downes. London: Charles and Edwin Layton.

Rao, C. Radhakrishna. 1964. Sir Ronald Aylmer Fisher — the architect of multivariate analysis. *Bilmetrics* 20:286-300.

Reid, D. D. 1972. Does inheritance matter in disease? The use of twin studies in medical research. In *Statistics: A Guide to the Unknown,* ed. J. M. Tanur, F. Mosteller, W. H. Kruskal, et al. pp. 77-83. San Francisco: Holden-Day.

Rothblatt, Sheldon. 1968. *The revolution of the dons: Cambridge and society in Victorian England.* New York: Basic Books.

Sampford, Michael R., ed. 1964. In memoriam Ronald Aylmer Fisher, 1890-1962. *Biometrics* 20:237-373.

Sarton, George. 1935. Quetelet. *Isis* 23:6-24.

————. (1936a) 1957a. The study of the history of mathematics. In *The Study of the History of Mathematics and the Study of the History of Science.* New York: Dover.

———. (1936b) 1957b. The study of the history of science. In *The Study of the History of Mathematics and the Study of the History of Science.* New York: Dover.

———. 1952. *A guide to the history of science.* Waltham, Mass.: Chronica Botanica Co.

Seal, Hilary L. (1967) 1970. The historical development of the Gauss linear model. In *Studies in the History of Statistics and Probability,* ed. E. S. Pearson and M. G. Kendall, vol. 1, pp. 207-230. London: Charles Griffin and Co.

———. 1968. Moivre, Abraham de. In *International Encyclopedia of the Social Sciences,* ed. David L. Sills, vol. 10, pp. 409-411. New York: Macmillan and The Free Press.

Senders, Virginia L. 1958. *Measurement and statistics.* New York: Oxford University Press.

Sheynin, O. B. (1968) 1970. On the early history of the law of large numbers. In *Studies in the History of Statistics and Probability,* ed. E. S. Pearson and M. G. Kendal, vol. 1, pp. 231-239. London: Charles Griffin and Co.

———. 1971. Studies in the history of probability and statistics. XXV. On the history of some statistical laws of distribution. *Biometrika* 58:234-236.

———. 1973. Mathematical treatment of astronomical observations (a historical essay). *Archive for History of Exact Sciences* 11:97-126.

———. 1977a. Laplace's theory of errors. *Archive for History of Exact Sciences* 17:1-61.

———. 1977b. Early history of the theory of probability. *Archive for History of Exact Sciences* 17:201-259.

Simpson, Thomas. 1755. A letter to the right honourable George Earl of Macclesfield, president of the Royal Society, on the advantage of taking the mean of a number of observations, in practical astronomy. *Phil. Trans. Roy. Soc. London* 49:82-93.

Smith, David Eugene. (1929) 1959. *A source book in mathematics,* vols. 1 and 2. New York: Dover.

Snedecor, George W. 1934. *Calculation and interpretation of analysis of variance and covariance.* Ames, Iowa: Collegiate Press.

———. (1937a) 1946. *Statistical methods applied to experiments in agriculture and biology.* 4th ed. Ames, Iowa: Collegiate Press.

———. (1937b) 1956. *Statistical methods applied to experiments in agriculture and biology.* 5th ed. Ames, Iowa: The Iowa State University Press.

Snow, C. P. 1967. Foreword. In *A Mathematician's Apology,* by G. H. Hardy, pp. 9-58. Cambridge: Cambridge University Press.

Soper, H. E.; Young, A. W.; Cave, B. M.; Lee, A. and Pearson, K. 1917. A cooperative study. On the distribution of the correlation coefficient in small samples. Appendix II to the papers of "Student" and Fisher. *Biometrika* 11:328-413.

"Sophister." 1928. Discussion of small samples drawn from an infinite skew population. *Biometrika* 20a:389-423.

Spence, Janet T.; Underwood, Benton J.; Duncan, Carl P.; and Cotton, John W. 1968. *Elementary statistics*. 2nd ed. New York: Appleton-Century-Crofts.

Spence, Janet T.; Cotton, John W.; Underwood, Benton J.; and Duncan, Carl P. 1976. *Elementary statistics*. 3rd ed. Englewood Cliffs, N.J.: Prentice-Hall.

Spencer Brown, G. 1957. *Probability and scientific inference*. London: Longman, Green and Co.

Spink, Wesley W. 1978. *Infectious disease: Prevention and treatment in the nineteenth and twentieth centuries*. Minneapolis: University of Minnesota Press.

Stanley, J. C. 1966. The influence of Fisher's "The Design of Experiments" on educational research thirty years later. *American Educational Research Journal* 3:223-229.

Stewart, Ian. 1977. Gauss. *Scientific American* 237, no. 1: 122-131.

Stigler, Stephen M. 1974. Gergonne's 1815 paper on the design and analysis of polynomial regression experiments. *Historia Mathematica* 1:431-447.

———. 1975. Napoleonic statistics: The work of Laplace. *Biometrika* 62:503-517.

———. 1977. An attack on Gauss, published by Legendre in 1820. *Historia Mathematica* 4:31-35.

Stimson, Dorothy. 1948. *Scientists and amateurs: A history of the Royal Society*. New York: Henry Schuman.

Stouffer, S. A. 1958. Karl Pearson — An appreciation on the 100th anniversary of his birth. *J. Am. Statist. Assoc.* 53:23-27.

Symonds, P. M. 1926. Variations of the product-moment (Pearson) coefficient of correlation. *Journal of Educational Psychology* 17:458-469.

Tanur, J. M.; Mosteller, F.; Kruskal, W. H.; et al. 1972. *Statistics: A Guide to the Unknown*. San Francisco: Holden-Day.

Taeuber, C. 1972. Information for the nation from a sample survey. In *Statistics: A Guide to the Unknown*, ed. J. M. Tanur, F. Mosteller, W. H. Kruskal, et al., pp. 285-296. San Francisco: Holden-Day.

Terman, L. M. 1917. The intelligence quotient of Francis Galton in childhood. *American Journal of Psychology* 28:209-215.

———. 1976. The great conspiracy. In *The IQ Controversy: Critical Readings*, ed. N. J. Block and G. Dworkin, pp. 30-38. New York: Pantheon Books.

Thiele, Joachim. 1969. Karl Pearson, Ernst Mach, John B. Stallo: Briefe aus den Jahren 1897 bis 1904. *Isis* 60:535-542.

Todhunter, Issac. (1865) 1949. *A history of the mathematical theory of probability from the time of Pascal to that of Laplace.* New York: Chelsea.

Todhunter, Issac, and Pearson, Karl. (1886-1893) 1960. *A history of the theory of elasticity and of the strength of materials, from Galilei to Lord Kelvin.* New York: Dover.

Ulam, S. M. 1976. *Adventures of a mathematician.* New York: Scribners.

U.S. Department of Health, Education, and Welfare. 1973. *Summary report: New Jersey graduated work incentive experiment.* Washington, D.C.

Underwood, Benton J.; Duncan, Carl P.; Taylor, Janet A.; and Cotton, John W. 1954. *Elementary statistics.* New York: Appleton-Century-Crofts.

Venn, John. 1888. *The logic of chance.* 3rd ed. London: Macmillan.

J. W. 1938. Obituary: William Sealy Gosset, 1876-1937. *J. Roy. Statist. Soc.* 101:249-250.

Walker, Helen M. 1929. *Studies in the history of statistical method, with special reference to certain educational problems.* Baltimore: Williams & Wilkins.

———. 1934. Abraham De Moivre. *Scripta Mathematica* 2:316-333.

———. 1968. Pearson, Karl. In *International Encyclopedia of the Social Sciences,* ed. David L. Sills, Vol. II, pp. 496-503. New York: Macmillan and The Free Press.

Walker, Helen M., and Lev, Joseph. 1953. *Statistical inference.* New York: Henry Holt.

Watson, Robert I., Sr. 1978. *The great psychologists.* 4th ed. Philadelphia: J. B. Lippincott Company.

Weaver, Warren. 1952. Statistics. *Scientific American* 186, no. 1:60-63.

Weinberg, George H., and Schumaker, John A. 1962. *Statistics: An intuitive approach.* Belmont, Calif.: Wadsworth Publishing Co., Inc.

Welch, B. L. 1958. "Student" and small sample theory. *J. Am. Statist. Assoc.* 53:777-788.

Weldon, W. F. R. 1890. The variation occurring in certain Decapod Crustacea. I. *Crangon vulgaris. Proc. Roy. Soc. London* 47:445-453.

———. 1892. Certain correlated variations in *Crangon vulgaris. Proc. Roy. Soc. London* 51:2-21.

———. 1893. On certain correlated variations in *Carcinus moenas. Proc. Roy. Soc. London* 54:318-329.

———. 1898. Presidential address to the Zoological Section of the British Association. *Report of the British Association for the Advancement of Science* 68:887-902.

Westergaard, Harald. 1932. *Contributions to the history of statistics.* London: P. S. King and Son, Ltd.

Westfall, Richard S. 1980. Newton's marvellous years of discovery and their aftermath: Myth versus manuscript. *Isis* 71:109-121.

White, Colin. 1964. Unkind cuts at statisticians. The American Statistician 18, no. 5:15-17.

Wilks, S. S. 1951. Undergraduate statistical education. J. Am. Statist. Assoc. 46:1-18.

Williams, Frederick. 1968. Reasoning with statistics: Simplified examples in communications research. New York: Holt, Rinehart, and Winston.

Wonnacott, Thomas H., and Wonnacott, Ronald J. 1977. Introductory statistics. 3rd ed. New York: John Wiley & Sons, Inc.

Wood, T. B., and Stratton, F. J. M. 1910. The interpretation of experimental results. J. Agr. Sci. 3:417-440.

Wright, R. L. D. 1976. Understanding statistics: An informal introduction for the behavioral sciences. New York: Harcourt Brace Javanovich.

Yamane, Taro. 1964. Statistics, an introductory analysis. New York: Harper & Row.

Yates, F. 1939. The comparative advantages of systematic and randomized arrangements in the design of agricultural and biological experiments. Biometrika 30:440-466.

————. 1964. Sir Ronald Fisher and the design of experiments. Biometrics 20: 307-321.

Yule, G. Udny. 1895. On the correlation of total pauperism with proportion of out-relief. I. All ages. Economic Journal 5:603-611.

————. 1896. On the correlation of total pauperism with proportion of out-relief. II. Males over sixty-five. Economic Journal 6:613-623.

————. 1897a. On the significance of Bravais' formulae for regression, etc., in the case of skew correlation. Proc. Roy. Soc. London 60:477-489.

————. 1897b. On the theory of correlation. J. Roy. Statist. Soc. 60:812-854.

————. 1900. On the association of attributes in statistics. Phil. Trans. Roy. Soc. London, Series A, 194:257-319.

————. 1922. On the application of the x^2 method to association and contingency tables, with experimental illustrations. J. Roy. Statist. Soc. 85:95-104.